At R

WRITING ON ~~AND OVER~~ THE
EDGE OF SOUTH AFRICA

At RISK

WRITING ON AND OVER THE EDGE OF SOUTH AFRICA

Edited by
Liz McGregor and Sarah Nuttall

JONATHAN BALL PUBLISHERS
Johannesburg & Cape Town

Published in 2007 by
JONATHAN BALL PUBLISHERS (PTY) LTD
PO Box 33977
Jeppestown
2043

ISBN 978-1-86842-271-5

Typesetting and reproduction by Etienne van Duyker, Cape Town
Set in 11 on 14 pt New Baskerville
Printed and bound by CTP Book Printers, Cape Town

Acknowledgements

Deborah Posel would like to thank Edwin Cameron, Mark Gevisser and Jonny Steinberg for astute readings of earlier drafts.

Graeme Reid would like to acknowledge that research on which his story is based was funded by the Netherlands Foundation for the Advancement of Tropical Research (WOTRO) of the Netherlands Organisation for Scientific Research (NOW).

Liz McGregor and Sarah Nuttall would like to warmly thank Deborah Posel for her discussions with us on all aspects of this manuscript.

It's been a pleasure working with Jeremy Boraine and Jane Rogers at Jonathan Ball Publishers and we thank them for their insight and care.

Contents

Foreword

The stories we tell each other, about ourselves, are part of what makes us who we collectively are. Our social being in the world is made up of narrative layers: some subterranean, some surfacing. Not all of them make it into the open. Some layers remain local, others form national narratives, and others travel abroad.

The kinds of stories that dominated the late apartheid period were tales of exile, struggle, community, resistance – fundamentally political narratives. The individual, in most of these stories, was either a hero or a traitor. Despite their complexity and range, these narratives depicted a world divided into good and evil. The aftermath of apartheid brought an explosion of stories of trauma, within a broader horizon of hope. This, in many respects, was what the Truth and Reconciliation Commission was about. Here, the storyteller was a witness, and the timescape dealt with was the immediate past. So, too, in the aftermath of the TRC, came the confessional – the work of expiation, the perspectives of victims and perpetrators.

What we see now, just beginning to cusp, is a second wave. This wave is formed from a groundswell of personal stories written in a range of registers across a distinctive set of social issues (AIDS, crime, new forms of migration and mobility, consumerism). Writers of the now draw on registers of the unexpected – surprise, shock, bewilderment – and these registers come to characterise a new narrative age. In some respects they draw into the open the idea that freedom is not what they though it would be; that it has brought unanticipated challenges. Writers write with a degree of astonishment – and especially with an alertness to a sense of risk. They take risks that they didn't or couldn't before – writerly risks, personal risks, professional risks. What we see too, in this second wave, are emerging registers of uncertainty, scepticism and doubt. These cohabit with an ongoing commitment by writers to the place in which they live – South Africa. The surfacing of scepticism and doubt emerges after a cultural moment of wonder at what was often referred to as a 'miracle' of political transition without bloodshed. We are living free, but with doubt – but also generally without demoralisation, writers seem to suggest.

The second wave is not entirely distinct from what has gone before. One wave carries the undertow of that which precedes it. But this surge of narrative energy is new, of the now, and it speaks in a voice not heard in South Africa before.

The nonfiction stories gathered here are written in the spirit of the second wave. They are written by academics and journalists but they collapse the distance that academic writing and journalism often impose. In academia or news writing, writers are expected to discount their personal reactions and to offer few, or no, private opinions. What is offered here, by contrast, are candid, intimate voices.

10

Most strikingly, these stories embrace the idea of risk. To take a risk is to embrace uncertainty; to accept the possibility of danger, distress, or disaster. It is also an inherently creative act: without taking a risk, there is no prospect of surprise, change or unexpected gain. Risk-taking can be unnerving and fearful, but can also be exhilarating. It is a way of taking on the unknown.

The narratives gathered here go below the surface to elicit the contours and forms of life in South Africa now. They are written by people born here and who have lived through enormous change in the last fifteen years – and those who have come to live here. The issues the stories probe are not the ones that drew us, like moths to a flame, a decade and a half ago. Most strikingly, perhaps, as the rise of AIDS creates a new narrative vortex, is the sense that death itself is happening in new ways – as stories by Liz McGregor and Deborah Posel suggest. McGregor, for instance, ventures into the conspiracy-laden realm of Modjadji, the late rain queen, who took unprecedented risks in relation to her royal position, to find out how and why she died. Posel tells a riveting story of the conjunction of freedom and death, and her unwitting complicity with the silences that envelop the HIV/AIDS epidemic.

Then, 'How do we live together (or at least next door)?' is a question that Graeme Reid, Makhosazana Xaba and Tom Odhiambo's stories each implicitly pose, in registers ranging from irony to whimsy to the risqué.

A third issue emerging from these stories is the na-scent question, 'What *are* the fruits of freedom?' The narratives by Jon Hyslop, Achille Mbembe and Justice Malala each offer a possible answer. While Hyslop risks a look at his past self, and the ideas that he and many on the white left once held, Mbembe reveals why, when he could have lived elsewhere, he chooses to live and work here. Malala is haunted by the image of a man at his window, gun in hand, wanting to take it all away.

For Lara Allen, Fred Khumalo and Jonny Steinberg, the question at the front of their writerly minds is, 'How to understand the lives of others?' Brenda Fassie, the elusive subject of Allen's piece, took risks in her music and with her life, and lived on the edge of social convention. Why she risked more than others, and what its consequences were, is the focus of Allen's tale. In a bar in Yeoville, an African migrant challenges Fred Khumalo to follow him into the night – to see where he sleeps. Khumalo leaves with him – and later tells his story. Steinberg writes about an intriguing episode which took place at Pollsmoor Prison. Why did the subject of his story take such an unthinkable risk?

Finally, to live in South Africa is to be subliminally primed for major loss, the most common causes being traffic accidents, crime or HIV/AIDS. Sarah Nuttall narrates her experience of a different kind of loss altogether, when her baby died in shocking circumstances.

What we suggest, then, is that the stories gathered in this book represent a new wave of South African narrative energy. Each is written with a high level of self-reflection, as they probe themes of living and dying, of freedom, otherness and loss. They speak for and of South Africa now, but they also speak to a series of elsewheres, as they probe questions that matter everywhere.

Each of the authors is closely associated with WISER (Wits Institute for Social and Economic Research).

Based in Johannesburg, WISER produces cutting-edge work on contemporary South Africa. It is an interactive space that produces academic work but also hosts journalists, writers and public intellectuals. Its public events attract many different audiences. In putting this book together, we chose stories that would fill a gap in the public arena. South Africa is still a country in which public discourse is thin. Seldom do we find stories that uncover the full complexity of the place; and too often we know that there are fascinating stories out there which don't get told.

Sarah Nuttall
Liz McGregor
Johannesburg 2007

Who Killed the Rain Queen?

Liz McGregor

Makobo, Queen Modjadji VI, first sparked my imagination when I read about her inauguration as rain queen in April 2003. She was young – only 25 – female, and ascribed the most beguiling of powers in a world beset by fears of global warming and environmental disaster. Modjadji, it was claimed, could control the rain.

There were salacious titbits: she was given a harem of wives. She could have as many lovers as she wanted but she could only procreate with a brother or cousin. The eldest daughter born of such a union would inherit the crown. In a patriarchal country like South Africa – and nowhere more so than the tradition-dominated rural areas – such female freedoms stood out.

I was not the only one drawn to the rain queen: Nelson Mandela himself flew up to Limpopo for the inauguration. He took the young royal under his wing, promising to send her to England for further education, and contributed a school, a tarred road up to the Royal Kraal and two luxury cars to ferry her about in the style to which she should become accustomed.

And then, just over two years later, on 12 June 2005, there was another flurry of publicity. Queen Modjadji was dead. A spontaneous fire had broken out in the kraal housing her coffin. Her brother had fled the country. Her baby daughter, now heir to the throne, had been kidnapped by the queen's lover, David Mohale, who claimed Makobo had been poisoned. His own and his baby daughter's lives were also in danger, he said.

I became increasingly intrigued. What had happened to this young, hopeful life? Who killed the rain queen?

*

I looked for books about her and found surprisingly little. She was first mythologised in literature by Rider Haggard in his novel *She,* written in 1887. The queen, mysteriously white, is so alluring that no man – not even the British adventurer hero, a self-confessed misogynist – can resist her.

Then, 50 years later, husband and wife anthropological team, EJ and JD Krige, produced a dense, seminal work on the rain queen and her ethnic group, the Balobedu. With a foreword by Krige's uncle, then Prime Minister, Jan Smuts, it describes an idyllic, prelapsarian community living in great harmony and relative prosperity, under an intricate and unique matrilineal social system. Presiding over this was the sacred queen, Modjadji, transformer of the clouds, whose power over rain afforded her the adoration of her people and the respect of neighbours.

In the intervening 60-odd years, there had been little of substance written about her, which was puzzling, given how much interest she evoked.

It was only when I personally tried to penetrate the realm of the rain queen that I understood why this might be the case.

*

The Modjadji area is in northeastern Limpopo, about a five-hour drive from Johannesburg. The nearest town is Modjadjikloof, itself about an hour's drive from the Royal Kraal. Until last year, the town was called Duiwelskloof. It was renamed in honour of Modjadji VI.

What are one's first impressions of the magical realm of the rain queen? Even in mid-July, the place appears startlingly fertile; a series of softly rolling green hills dotted with houses. Modern brick homes with tin roofs stand side by side with traditional mud rondavels. Everywhere are banana, pawpaw and mango trees, their fruit still embryonic but rich with the promise of a good harvest. People gather in twos and threes on the edges of the road. Strings of schoolchildren still in their uniforms saunter along, clearly in no hurry to get home.

Is this lushness, this evidence of abundant rain, the reason that Modjadji's legend remains so powerful? Particularly in this part of the world, where drought is so pervasive and so destructive, rain means food. It means life. One could see why the sudden death of the transformer of the clouds would seem so catastrophic: why it might be seen as curse on an entire people. And why someone would need to be blamed for it.

The tarred road to the Royal Kraal – Mandela's gift – winds up steeply, with a sharp drop to a valley on one side. The mountain side is dotted with the odd spaza shop, housed in small wooden structures, selling tomatoes, avocados, nuts and cabbages. After a five-minute drive, you're in Modjadji: the first building is a pretty little white Lutheran church; alongside it is the Bolobedu Primary School with colourful murals painted on the low outside wall and a sprawl of purple bougainvillea. Next comes the clinic, a large, face-brick building. And then a little further along is an open piece of ground which serves as a parking lot for customers of the Modjadji Tavern. Beyond that is the hidden world of the Royal Kraal, unsignposted and off limits to outsiders.

The only place for visitors to stay that is anywhere near the Royal Kraal is the Modjadji African Ivory Route camp, a cluster of traditional rondavels in the middle of the ancient cycad forest. It's a magical place: the cycads, many over twelve metres tall and a century old, form giant green canopies over a forest full of duikers, vervet monkeys, bushpigs and waterbuck. On my first research trip I stayed there but, because one needs to book out the entire camp, I had to look for an alternative for future visits. One of the guides at the camp was Josephine Modjadji, a 42-year-old mother of five to whom I took an instant liking. She was bright, engaging and, best of all, related to the royal family. I gave her a lift home one evening and discovered that she lived in a substantial brick house on top of the mountain with a stunning view over the valley below. Would it be possible to board with her on future visits, I asked, and she could double as my host and guide on her days off from the Ivory

Route camp. She jumped at the chance. Her dream, she revealed, was to build a B & B on the plot next to her house in time for 2010 when, she hoped, foreign visitors would flock to Modjadji.

*

I arrived for my next visit a month or so later in happy anticipation of many mutually productive hours in Josephine's company. She had grown up in the Royal Kraal. Her mother still lived there. Josephine herself had been a close friend of Makobo's mother. I would gain an insider's view on the shenanigans of the royal family while, in return, dispensing tips on what European tourists might like for breakfast and how their rooms should be decorated (a touch of Afro-chic, I thought – the odd drum and maybe a portrait of the rain queen, with a Modjadji cycad or two in the garden).

I was convinced Josephine was onto a winner. The view over the cycad forest was inspirational. Organic produce – fertilised only by the purest cow dung – sprang wild from the hillside: huge spinach leaves oozing iron and protein sprouted among pawpaw, litchi, naartjie and avocado trees. This natural, chemical-free fare, combined with the magical legend of the rain queen, would, I thought, be hugely attractive to the more sophisticated tourist.

It didn't take me long to discover what a naive fool I was.

Often, working as a journalist in South Africa, it is one's self who poses the difficulty. The fact that I am white, female, middle-class and speak only two of the eleven official languages with any proficiency inevitably influences my interaction with people of other races or the opposite gender. In Modjadji, it is the opacity of the system itself which creates the barrier. It does not want to be fully known, not even to its own people. Even the language of this small, incestuous tribe – about 400 000 in all – speaks to this. There is no written form of Khelovedu, the language spoken by the Balobedu. The most common words used in response to any question about the royal family are: 'It's a secret.'

I had thought my question was a fairly straightforward one, easily answered. How did Makobo die? In fact, I got many contradictory answers, most of them bolstering various conspiracy theories.

At the time of my first arrival in Modjadji in July 2006, the status quo was thus: the precipitate death of Makobo, Queen Modjadji VI, had exacerbated a bitter power struggle between rival factions in the ruling oligarchy over who was to be appointed regent until it could be claimed by Masalanabo, Makobo's baby daughter and heir to the throne. Traditionally the Royal Council which governs the realm's affairs was comprised of four members from each of five royal families. One family, the Mokotos, wanted to appoint Julia Mabale, Makobo's mother's half-sister and a lecturer at the University of the North. The remaining four, under the leadership of one John Malatji, wanted Mpapatla, Makobo's 25-year-old brother, to be regent. The wild card in all this was David Mohale, who had disappeared with his baby daughter, Masalanabo. He rejected both Julia Mabale and Mpapatla as regents.

In the meantime, John Malatji had installed himself in the offices of the Modjadji Traditional Authority opposite the Royal Kraal and appeared to be in de facto control. He was going ahead with the grooming of Mpapatla as regent, and the latter's first public appearance would be presiding over the rain-making ceremonies which were to begin in the first weekend of October, the beginning of spring.

There is another whole cast of characters who are invisible – the ancestral spirits who play a profound role in Modjadji life. Chief amongst these are the dead queens. Later, I was to discover their power.

The setting for this drama was the Royal Kraal, called Khethakoni, which was established by Modjadji III in 1895, about the same time that Rider Haggard wrote *She*. The Royal Kraal occupies a large piece of land mostly hidden from view. From the top one can see in the distance a large pink house, surrounded by lawn and cycad palms. This is the palace, home to successive rain queens and now to the putative regent, Mpapatla. Notices attached to the high fence surrounding it warn intruders off. Even taking photographs from the road felt risky. I added a tour of the Royal Kraal to the list of requests I would put to Josephine. Top of the list was an invitation to a rain-making ceremony. After that came various interviews: with Mpapatla and with Makobo's former friends and family.

I put this list to Josephine, who shook her head. Nothing was possible without the permission of John Malatji, who happened to be her cousin. She phoned him to set up an appointment. He promised to come round to the house. Josephine herself would not utter a word about the royal family until Malatji had given his blessing.

By late evening, Malatji still hadn't come. And he had stopped answering his phone. By the following morning, I was beginning to fear I was wasting my time when a visitor tap-tapped his way into Josephine's yard. It was a friend of hers, a blind man called Justice Mokhwaripa who, Josephine told me excitedly, knew everything there was to know about Lobedu culture. I had learnt by now to be slightly disingenuous: any direct question about Makobo was met with that infuriating phrase: 'It's a secret.' Easier to start with general questions. My quest for the moment, then, was to explore Lobedu history.

Josephine settled Justice down on a plastic chair under the peach tree and brought him a plate of pap and relish. When he had finished eating, he did indeed tell me Lobedu history. It roughly correlated with the history given by the Kriges but here is as good a place as any to tell it: the rain queen is a direct descendant of Monomotapa, rain-maker and mighty monarch of Zimbabwe, responsible for that ancient architectural miracle, the Great Zimbabwe. Monomotapa's crown passes to his son, Mambo, who has a daughter called Dzugudini. Although unmarried she falls pregnant. Mambo wants to punish her seducer but Dzugudini won't reveal his name. It is thought to be her brother. To protect him, Dzugudini's mother feverishly teaches her daughter rain-making skills and steals the rain charms and sacred beads for her. Dzugudini and her baby son flee south. By virtue of her incestuous act, Dzugudini justifies the creation of a new people, eventually to become the Balobedu of northeast Limpopo.

For 200 years, the Balobedu were ruled by a king. Around 1800, this switched to a queen because the then king, Mogodo, fell out with his sons and decided to make his daughter, Modjadji, his queen. He had a daughter with her and from then, the eldest daughter of the queen inherited the throne. The headmen of her realm brought her their daughters to be her wives. These were called *vatanuni*. All their children belonged to the queen but she procreated only with a close relative – a brother or a cousin chosen by the Royal Council – in order to keep the bloodline pure. He entered her palace in the dead of night and left before dawn. The queen did not have a normal marital relationship.

Makobo, the first queen to ascend the throne in the 21st century and in modern, democratic South Africa, said: 'To hell with all this. I will choose the father of my children and I will live the way I want to.'

This did not go down well.

'She didn't follow the demands of the culture,' said Justice sorrowfully. 'She drank. She visited hotels. She went wrong.' Makobo's worst crime was to have invited her lover, David Mohale, to live with her in the pink palace. And it was on Mohale that the ire of the community was heaped. 'One can't be angry with the queen,' explained Justice. 'So they blamed Mohale.'

*

And then, a message arrived from Malatji. There was another hoop to jump through. A verbal request for an interview was not good enough. I had to submit it in writing. With no alternative readily available, I tore a page from my notebook and wrote out a formal request. I took it down to the tribal office, a relic from the apartheid days of Bantu administration. Later a response was delivered to Josephine's house:

Madam,

1. We believe a proper procedure for you would be to direct your request in writing to the Royal Council in advance of travelling to Khethakoni and give the Royal Council an ample time to consider your request and respond timeously to you …
2. In the times in which we live we have met conmen and conwomen and got hurt. We have to proceed with caution …

The letter went on to say that, nevertheless, I was granted a preliminary audience with the Royal Council the following day at 8 am.

John Malatji and two other members of the Royal Council were waiting for me. Malatji, sitting at the centre of the table, was clearly in charge. He had grown up in the Royal Kraal but much of his adult life had been spent as a big fish in much larger ponds. He had been both director-general of Limpopo and vice rector of the University of the North. He spent the first ten minutes roundly berating me for my impudence in simply turning up and asking to meet the regent. The fact that I had directed my request through Josephine, an official tour guide and a member of the royal family, seemed irrelevant.

'If I walked into Buckingham Palace and said I wanted to see the queen, it would not work,' he thundered. 'There are certain etiquettes and conventions. We have a tradition that says the regent is not a tourist item.'

From this and one subsequent conversation, he confirmed what Justice had told me. As soon as she is enthroned, the queen theoretically transcends gender. 'No-one sees her as a woman. Being a man means power, authority, wealth and influence.' The fathers of the queen's children have no claim on their children, said Malatji. 'We know all the guys who've fathered royal children but none of them is father to them officially. The queen today makes her own choices but the children will not have the identity of the father. If they did and she made a wrong choice, she would have to step down.'

Mohale, said Malatji, was attempting to destroy tradition by claiming rights over Masalanabo, the fledgling queen. 'It's as if he is the regent for the little girl who is going to succeed her mother. And he can't be the regent.'

Mpapatla was the regent, said Malatji, and he would be in charge of Modjadji affairs until Masalanabo turned eighteen. I asked again to see Mpapatla. 'He's not a tourist item,' said Malatji firmly.

Throughout this interview I felt deeply uncomfortable. Malatji's initial dressing-down combined with the fact that he was flanked by two cohorts who barely spoke but were clearly in his thrall made me feel distinctly wrong-footed. Three large black men and one smallish white woman. Race, as ever in this country, came into it. I tried feebly to use it to my advantage.

'Is it because I'm white that you won't let me see him?'

But Malatji was much too smart to fall into that trap. It was nothing to do with race, he insisted. And I believed him.

'Have you read Rider Haggard's book *She*? It's about this place and you will find the sentence: "She who must not be seen." And what it means is that access to her is not an ordinary happening. It's a special happening. And it's not because you're hiding anything. It's because it's tradition. Traditional power lies in being not ordinary. If you go into shebeens and you're seen running a relationship in public and the like, your leadership is going to collapse in a matter of weeks. Your subjects will stop respecting you.

'Then we become defensive, protective. But she also knows that her power depends on us maintaining that. I mean, if she arrived here, we would all fall on the ground and not look at her. We'd ask you to throw yourself on the ground in recognition of her power. Now the regent, who is 25 years old, if he arrived here, we wouldn't talk to him as a young man. We would talk to him as "He who must be obeyed. He who must not be seen."'

What about developing Modjadji as a tourist destination, I asked, thinking of Josephine and her dreams of a B & B.

There had to be a balance, he said, between opening up to tourism and maintaining cultural integrity. 'We can't organise ourselves to be only a tourist destination,' he said. 'It would be too expensive a price to pay. We have a tradition that is very strong and if you dump it, you don't have it any more.

'We grow but we grow our own way. We had an educated queen. She drove herself. She did her own shopping. She had an Internet bank account. She spoke English. She had friends around the world.'

This seemed a good opening for questions about her death but I feared that doing so would transgress another invisible boundary. I still very much wanted to attend a rain-making ceremony but that clearly depended on the goodwill of these men.

'Do you still want to go and interview the regent?' interrupted Malatji, and then answered himself. 'We don't think you should. What do you want there? We're trying to give the answers the regent will give you.'

No, I no longer needed to see the regent, I agreed, despising myself for my cowardice. But I would love to attend a rain-making ceremony.

'Put your request in writing,' said Malatji.

*

I thought about his analogy with the British royal family. In fact, within her own world, Queen Modjadji had more clout than her British counterpart. The British sovereign's realm might dwarf that of the rain queen, but the latter retains something the former long ago

ceded to an elected government: political and economic power. The rain queen still holds title to all Lobedu
land. Traditional courts function under her sway. No
development can go ahead without her signature. No
wonder so many powerful men were keen to get close
to Queen Modjadji VI. And why they resented Mohale's
influence over her.

*

Back in Johannesburg, I wrote an obsequious letter to
Malatji, asking for another interview, in the hope that
more doors would be opened to me, and for permission to attend a rain-making ceremony. I had by now
acquired a phone number for David Mohale but his
phone was always switched off. I made another trip to
Modjadji.

Again, Josephine tried to persuade Malatji to come
round. Again he said he would try. Again we waited in
vain. I had, however, made contact with a local freelance
reporter who claimed he could help me find David
Mohale. I arranged to meet him in Modjadji and together we set off up an impossibly primitive road to find
a friend of Mohale's who apparently knew his address.
This led us to the nearby town of Kgapane and, after
several wrong turns, we arrived at a square suburban
house. Bingo. It was Mohale's parents' house. We found
his brother at home who said Mohale himself was in Pretoria. I left my phone number and took the numbers of
Mohale's brother and cousin. I was getting closer.

*

By now, I had begun to form a picture of Makobo's life. She was born in 1978 to Maria Khethukhunya when the latter was only sixteen years old. Her father – and that of Mpapatla – was a cousin of her mother's. Maria, according to John Malatji, drank heavily. In 1989, Maria died of cancer and the children were sent to live with an aunt, Julia Mabale, in neighbouring Kgapane. It was Julia Mabale whom the Mokoto wing of the royal family wanted installed as regent instead of Mpapatla.

Because Julia Mabale herself only had sons, she entrusted Makobo to yet another relative who had daughters living with her. Makobo later complained that this relative treated her like a servant and she was so loaded with household chores that she had little time for her schoolwork. But she completed her matric at Makgoka High School and later went to study further at a vocational college. Mpapatla, meanwhile, was sent to Manorvlei Primary, a farm school in Tzaneen, where he was registered under a false name. This was apparently both for his own safety and to ensure he was treated as a normal child and did not grow up with any delusions of grandeur.

These are the facts. Less easy to confirm are reports about Makobo's behaviour. I was told by various sources in Modjadji that Makobo was a wild child. She drank at shebeens, danced at discos. She had boyfriends. She drank. She took drugs. She was '*stout*' (naughty), as one person put it.

She certainly had sex: while still a teenager, she gave birth to a son. He is now seven years old and in good health. One rumour has it that this relationship also precipitated her death. The father of her son, it is said, later died of AIDS, which he could have passed on to her.

Another bit of information, which I found particularly fascinating, was that she dressed like a man. Even before she became queen and officially transcended the limitations of her sex, Makobo was experimenting with representations of gender. She wore big men's shirts and men's trousers, I was told. She refused to wear hair extensions or braid her hair. Instead, she kept it in its natural state: short and curly. Sometimes, she covered it with a sporty, the hat favoured by trendy township youths.

*

Justice Mokhwripa, the blind poet, became pretty much a constant fixture during my visits, stationed on his chair under the peach tree, poring over voluminous Braille documents. He appeared to be on the mailing list for most governmental departments' annual reports which, commendably, all seem to be translated into Braille. Every now and again, he would entertain us with exciting snippets, such as: 'Did you know that thirteen South Africans died in the Asian tsunami?'

One morning a few days before the rain-making ceremonies were due to begin, he came tap-tapping into the yard with more exciting news: he had just heard on the community radio that Mpapatla was in the Polokwane Medi-Clinic ICU with serious injuries after a car crash sustained ten days before. All my own feelings of entitlement as a member of a democratic society were outraged. The local newspaper, the *Capricorn News*, had just featured a front-page story announcing that Mpa-patla was to lead the rain-making ceremonies in his first public appearance as the regent. In other words, as the leader of people such as Justice and Josephine. They lived metres from the Royal Kraal; Josephine was in and out of her mother's house there. Yet she had to hear about such an important development from the radio, ten days after the event. Ancient official reports in Braille for the blind seemed an appropriate metaphor. I tried to stir up indignation. 'You are paying R10 a household to this man,' I said. 'He is supposed to be your leader. You are entitled to be told if he has been in a serious car accident.'

'Everything about the royal family is a secret,' replied Josephine, as usual. Then she added: 'It's muti. Someone is cursing them.'

She and Justice suggested I visit a local sangoma and I happily concurred: anything to relieve the tedium of waiting and, besides, maybe she could give me a traditional explanation for the queen's death. I kept hearing that she had died because she had infuriated the ancestors by flouting traditional ways: they had withdrawn protection and she had therefore been vulnerable to attack from any source. It fitted the poison theory. It also fitted the perception that there had been a resurgence in witchcraft, particularly in rural areas, since the ending of apartheid. The sudden flowering of opportunities and resources had created intense competition and jealousy. Makobo, as queen, was rain-maker in more than just the literal sense. She also had it within her power to make certain individuals rich.

The three of us – me, Justice and Josephine – set off in my little car up some appalling roads. When we could drive no further, we got out and walked down an indistinct path, me leading the blind man, trying to follow Josephine's instructions shouted from behind. Eventually we ended up in a courtyard neatly decorated in cow dung with a rondavel in each corner. An ancient woman sat on a chair in the sun and an equally ancient man sat at the opposite end of the courtyard, Zimmer frame close by. Soon a couple of boys arrived, curious about the visitors, and they were ordered to bring chairs for us. Justice stated the reason for our visit. I wanted to visit the sangoma to cure myself of a run of bad luck (mostly around trying to get information about their royalty, although I didn't say so). The sangoma asked for R100. 'They see a white person and double the charge,' said Justice sorrowfully. 'A white person will bring me bad luck,' she grumbled. The old lady went into one of the huts and beckoned me to follow. First I had to take off my shoes. After a couple of minutes' argument, Justice and Josephine were allowed to follow me in. I sat on the floor opposite her and she placed a reed mat between us, onto which she threw a bagful of objects: small bones, ivory dominoes and sea shells. She asked what my totem animal was and when I said I didn't have one, she announced I was a crocodile. There was trouble waiting for me just behind the door, she said. Then she looked down and muttered something. Then she announced that she had dismissed the source of my trouble. All this was translated by Josephine and Justice, who periodically broke out into fits of giggles. I did not get the sense that they were taking all this terribly seriously.

I said: 'Tell me about the queen. Why did she die?'

The old woman instantly became quite histrionic. 'If I tell you the secrets of the royal family, I will be arrested and put in jail,' she cried, holding up both hands joined at the wrist.

*

And then David Mohale phoned. His tone was guarded, suspicious. I explained why I wanted to meet with him and he said he would come to Wits. I specified the Dulce Café in Senate House, thinking it would be easier to find than my office. I waited and waited and he didn't turn up. His phone was, as usual, switched off.

A few days later, he sent an SMS. Could I deposit R300 into his account? It seemed reasonable to ask for travel expenses if he was coming down from Kgapane so I transferred the money. Again we made a date and again he didn't turn up. At first I put his elusiveness down to unreliability. But I came to understand that it was fear that kept him on the run.

One afternoon, as I was leaving campus, my phone rang. It was David. He was at WISER.

Delighted, I ushered him into my office. He was tall and carried a fair amount of weight without being fat. He was wearing a black baseball cap, blue jeans and a faded, checked shirt. He filled my modest visitor's chair, legs splayed, a self-confident man. The reason he never answered his phone, he said, was that it had been used to deliver death threats. But now that he had decided to trust me, he was totally open.

David Mohale had spent sixteen years – more than half his adult life – in the United States. Born in 1963, he grew up in Kgapane but became involved in anti-apartheid activism while still at school and had to leave the country. He spent time in Botswana and Zimbabwe before taking up a scholarship to study in the US. In 1998, he was summoned home by his family to attend a funeral. An ANC stalwart, he got a job as manager of the Modjadjiskloof municipality, which encompassed the entire Modjadji area. Vast changes were taking place in governance at this time: under apartheid, facilities such as clinics, schools and roads had mostly been paid for by taxes levied on the local population by traditional leaders. Now taxes were paid to the ANC government and facilities provided through local municipalities, such as the one run by Mohale. Traditional leaders like Modjadji were no longer supposed to raise taxes from their people. The Modjadji area is now more than adequately provided with schools, clinics and an excellent regional hospital, all paid for by the state. Most homes have electricity, although water supply has been slower. David Mohale would have been the face of these modern miracles. And it was in this guise of provider that he met Makobo. She, in turn, was playing the part of the caring traditional leader, in touch with her people and their needs.

Mohale described their meeting. 'It was in 2001. I was at a suboffice in Kgapane and I was approached by some women. They asked if I, as municipal manager, could assist someone in one village who had lost his house.'

One of the women was Makobo and it was she whom

Mohale chose to take him to see the hapless villager. He claims that, although she looked familiar, he did not know who she was. It was instinct that made him select her above the others.

'I chose her from amongst those girls because I just felt that I know this person although I don't know her. We left for Modjadjiskloof and she told me she had actually dreamed about me. That made me very much interested. We went to the village and arranged assistance. The following day I went for myself to see what was happening and she was there. And after the tent had been erected and some supplies given to those people, we left. Then we became friends.'

Of course, they became more than friends. There can be little doubt that Makobo was very much in love with Mohale: she risked everything to be with him and their relationship survived for five years, despite intense pressure to break it off. One can imagine his appeal for her: he was more than a decade older. He was tall and handsome and had the exotic whiff of his sixteen years of American living.

When Makobo was crowned rain queen in April 2003, Mohale moved into the pink palace with her. He presents her as vulnerable, in need of his protection: 'When I met her, there was lots of danger around her; of witchcraft and poisoning,' he said.

'Many people have died in that house. You have seen that house and that yard – you have seen how big it is. Living there alone with the children, you might be afraid. If a man entered that property, what would the queen do? She needed someone who could protect her. When I was there, people never came into that yard.'

More controversially, he also set himself up as gate-keeper against the various men who came soliciting her approval for projects.

She was wooed by the most powerful men in the province, alleged Mohale, and the fact that she chose him above them infuriated them. Was it because she was so devastatingly attractive, I asked.

Oh no, he said, it was all to do with money. The queen's signature was needed for any development. 'Tenders. They wanted tenders. There were promises to build factories, industries. One man wanted her to list all her wealth, all her property and sign it over to a trust, but this man would be the founder of the trust. If, as now, she is deceased, everything would have been lost to that man.

'You must remember that all these people were academically superior to the queen so they could manipulate her. Some people were rejected because I told the queen not to sign.'

This is what provoked such intense anger against the couple and led to a campaign of persecution against them. 'She lived a short life under severe, depressing, strenuous opposition,' he said.

He was convinced she had been murdered by being poisoned. He himself at one point showed signs of having being poisoned, he said. 'I went to a doctor after I developed symptoms like vomiting and diarrhoea. The doctor assisted me.'

Could AIDS not have killed Makobo? I asked. I said I had been told the father of her child had died of AIDS, which made it quite possible he could have passed the virus on to her. After all, the cause of death on her death certificate was given as meningitis, an infection which often attacks people with a highly compromised immune system.

Mohale vigorously rejected this. There was no proof, he said, that the father of Makobo's son had died of AIDS. 'I think they are just trying to make him a scapegoat. It's all rumour and speculation, designed to convince the public to look the other way and not to look for the true cause.'

He believed the other reason the AIDS theory was being put about was in order to pre-empt suspicion should his baby daughter die suddenly. 'They will try to say the child died of some strange illness that killed the mother. Do you see what I am saying? But the child is healthy, is happy. There is no problem with the child.'

Stories about Makobo's wildness were part of this smear campaign, he claimed.

'She liked having fun before she became queen.' But, essentially, he said, she was a responsible person, strongly aware of her duties as traditional leader. She was also very religious, mixing her traditional beliefs with loyalty to the Zion Christian Church. 'She was a Good Samaritan. I met her as a result of a good deed, after all. After she became queen, she wore traditional clothes. And she went to church, the ZCC, which is very strict. You don't smoke, you don't drink, you must be honest. She was very strict. She believed that things must be done the right way.'

David Mohale was not a traditionalist. A very modern South African, he pinned his colours to the constitution. 'I fought for democracy,' he said. 'I did not fight for this country to become a chief. I was just drawn into these things because of my relationship with the queen.

'I don't undermine tradition. I believe these things are as important as the people involved with them believe them to be. The people can choose whether to follow them or not. Traditional authorities must exist within the parameters of the constitution.'

The constitution, he pointed out, protected his rights over his daughter, even if he and her mother were not married.

He had no patience with accusations that Makobo broke with tradition by allowing him to live with her. 'She did nothing wrong,' he said. 'She is the head of tradition so she can alter tradition.'

Poor Makobo, I thought. If she is indeed looking down on us from some better place, she must still be tormented. Her realm in chaos; her lover and her child on the run, in fear for their lives.

Where is Masalanabo now, I asked Mohale. He hesitated for a second, before replying that she was living somewhere remote from Modjadji, with a white Christian family. She was safe, he said.

What did he want for his daughter? 'Education,' he said. 'To be protected. To live a safe life. To one day grow up and then become what she wants. Right now, I'm obligated to defend her interests in respect to her mother but when she grows up she must make her own decision about whether she likes those things or not.'

As he left, he asked if I had a house or an apartment. Yes, I said. Well, maybe Masalanabo could come and spend a few days with me at some point, he said. I said

I'd be honoured to have her but it did strike me as a bit desperate, even to contemplate entrusting one's little girl to a virtual stranger.

*

On my next trip up north, I stopped off at the Limpopo Medi-Clinic, the private hospital in Polokwane where Makobo died. All they could tell me there was that she had died, surrounded by her ladies in waiting. But they did direct me to her physician, who practised from a suburban house in one of Polokwane's broad, jacaranda-lined streets.

The doctor, a middle-aged Afrikaans man with a shock of grey hair, explained that medical ethics prevented him from discussing Makobo's case specifically but he could tell me that he saw many cases where AIDS was so far advanced that there was nothing he could do. Cryptococcal meningitis was typically a presenting illness for those in the last stages of AIDS and invariably turned out to be fatal. I took this to mean that Makobo had had AIDS.

At various points in my research – and this was one of them – I became hugely disillusioned with the Balobedu. I thought it was all about a few people using tradition in a mad scramble for power and money. And that Makobo had lost her life to it. Even if it was AIDS she had died of, she was clearly so beset by fear of poisoning that she accepted constant ill health as her lot. And why was she not properly taken care of by the legions of people who professed to pay homage to her? Why was she not taken to doctors and given antiretrovirals before it was too late? Even if she were not actively killed, she was allowed to die. And that seemed to me to be a crime in itself.

*

After I'd been home for a few days, Josephine called. She was in a state of high distress. 'We have just buried my brother's son,' she said. 'He was poisoned by another man because he was jealous. Mpapatla had asked him to cook for him and wash his clothes.'

The boy had gone for a drink after the conversation with Mpapatla. Shortly afterwards, he became very ill. He was healthy and then he died.

Malignant jealousy, secrecy and fear: it seemed in my jaundiced state to sum up the Balobedu.

*

And then I went to a rain-making ceremony.

There had been no response to my letter asking to attend one so I had all but given up. Josephine, however, was determined. All her integrity and reputation as Modjadji's top tourist guide seemed to rest on getting me into a rain-making ceremony. The third ceremony in the sequence of five due to take place that spring was scheduled for 28 October. The final two were open only to the royal family so this one was my last chance. Phone Malatji, Josephine kept urging me in the preceding week. I kept phoning but got voice mail. Three days before the ceremony, I finally got hold of him. He said he would need to consult the Royal Council but would call me back. He didn't. On the Thursday evening, I finally got through to him. Permission had been granted! I set off for Modjadji the next day with Julia, a German anthropologist colleague. Josephine was on duty at the African Ivory Route camp so it was decided we should stay there. We braaied outside under a starry sky on the Friday evening and went to bed early.

During the night, a light rain fell, the first that spring, we were told. It was a good omen. We drove up to the Royal Kraal and parked outside the Modjadji Tavern. Josephine led us down a path along the lower boundary of the Royal Kraal to her mother's house. We were told to take off our shoes and then led through a series of courtyards to an open patch on the edge. Everywhere we went, females of varying ages, from very small girls to old women, were vigorously sweeping with brushes made from local straw. There was clearly a major spring-cleaning in progress. In the cooking courtyard were several large black galvanised-iron cooking pots, balanced over wood fires. Young boys were bringing crates full of startled looking white chickens. More women arrived, with sacks of tomatoes and enormous cabbages. They settled themselves on a low brick wall and began slicing away at the cabbages till mounds of delicate white slivers collected in yet more basins. Julia and I thought we could get away with just watching, especially when the chickens were hauled down a nearby slope by a lady with a large knife. But Josephine came over: 'They want you to cut cabbages,' she said. We were each given one of those vast cabbages, a knife and a basin and proceeded to hack away, attempting vainly to produce the same delicate slivers as our neighbours.

Josephine called us: 'The sacred cow is in the *kgoro*. Come. Come.' We dropped the cabbages and followed her as fast as our bare feet would allow to the *kgoro*, a bare, circular patch of ground the size of a small football field. In earlier days, this used to function as the royal court and it was still the site for traditional ceremonies, such as this. It was lined with sharpened branches about eight metres high. A corridor at the other end led out to the parking lot and the Modjadji Tavern.

John Malatji was in charge of a group of men attempting to separate a black calf from a herd of four or five cows. The calf kicked and bucked. She was not keen to be caught. But she had been identified as the sacred cow in a sangoma's dream and her destiny was decided. Eventually she was tethered by a rope to a pole in the center of the *kgoro*, which had now filled up with members of the extended royal family. Two old women arrived with gourds full of a thick, brown liquid. They opened paper bags and poured black powder into it. One of the old women muttered something and then poured beer into a flattish bowl which was held up to the cow, whose mouth was pushed into it. After a bit of a struggle, the cow drank some of the liquid and everyone cheered. I was told that the beer was sacred, its ingredients a secret passed down through generations. I knew there was no point in even asking what they were.

We repaired to a courtyard within the kraal and everyone sat on the ground. A flat-topped cylindrical object, about half a metre high, was built into the corner of the courtyard. This, said Malatji, who settled himself down next to us, was the Molekwane rain shrine. Beneath it was buried all manner of bones and other sacred objects. A spear and a necklace of blue beads lay on top. The same old woman as before crouched beside it, chanting, and then poured more sacred beer from the gourd onto the shrine.

This seemed to me a poignant moment. The old woman performing the sacred rites was merely a stand-in. This was the rain queen's job. It should have been Makobo anointing the shrine with the sacred beer.

I looked at John Malatji, sitting next to me, and thought that, even for him, this must represent something of a disappointment. He had wanted Mpapatla to conduct the ceremony, evidence that he had been successfully installed as regent. But Mpapatla too had been hit by misfortune. The injuries to his leg sustained during his most recent car accident had put him out of the running as well.

The children had gathered around the shrine and were licking the beer that had seeped onto the ground. The gourd was being passed among the adults. Each person had to take a sip and then put the gourd back onto the ground. The next person would then pick it up, take a

sip and put it down again. Drinking the beer after someone had passed it to you meant the source was human,
rather than divine. I took a sip when it reached me. The
beer was bitter and grainy. Millet seeds, apparently.

Malatji, relaxed and genial now, offered to show us
around the Royal Kraal. He led us through a maze of
footpaths separating various homesteads. Brick houses
with tile or corrugated-iron roofs were interspersed
with traditional rounded mud and dung rondavels,
some flanked by narrow, walled verandas. Avocado,
pawpaw and coral trees with their vivid scarlet blossoms
grew everywhere. It struck me here, as it so often does
in Modjadji, that, despite the lack of jobs, most people
look healthy, glossy, prosperous even. But, particularly
here in the Royal Kraal, one also had a sense of a confident middle class, although many of them were from
the Lobedu diaspora, returned for this most crucial
of rituals.

It made me think again about the value of ethnic
pride; of a cohesive, rooted community. The Balobedu
have often compared themselves to Jews or Muslims
when challenged about the inwardness of their culture.
It works for them, said the Balobedu. And it works for us.

Malatji had by now led us into another royal courtyard, empty except for an ancient woman with glasses so
thick one could barely identify her eyes behind them.
She emerged suddenly from the doorway of a hut with
the ferocity of a bulldog and proceeded to bark at Malatji
in Khelovedu. 'She is telling me I can't take you any further,' he said ruefully. 'The rest is secret.'

But he showed us, through a gap in the houses, a triangle of traditional huts in the distance. This was sacred territory, he said, where queens once lived and where sacred objects are buried; where the brews for rituals such as this were created. The old woman watched suspiciously from her doorway, making sure we didn't go any further. Higher up the hill was the pink palace, where queens lived and died. That too was forbidden territory.

Back at the Molekwane shrine, Malatji grew ever more expansive. Only the men were there now, sitting on benches, drinking ordinary traditional beer.

The conversation came back to Makobo and David Mohale. 'In the old days,' he said, 'the boyfriend would be slaughtered when she ascended the throne. Lovers must be a well-guarded secret. Anyone who talks about it would be lynched. If he is secretive, it will last. If he is open about it – in the old days, a team would be assembled to slaughter him. Now we just kick him out.'

Later, referring specifically to Mohale, he said. 'We were organising to lynch him.'

And about the baby, Masalanabo: 'She must grow up here. Mohale does have custody but we have guardianship. Otherwise, we will dethrone her.'

I had thought Mohale was a bit paranoid. I no longer thought so.

As the afternoon wore on, the old women brought out two big drums and placed them next to the shrine. These were the rain drums, brought out every year especially for this ritual. One was placed on its side, the other upright. They started playing, one beating the upright drum with both hands; the other with a stick. It was a steady, hypnotic rhythm. People formed a circle around the drums and shrine and shuffled around it, chanting. Every couple of beats, they stepped in unison towards the centre and clapped. It felt ancient and well-practised and, well, unknowable. I was enchanted by it.

Josephine came up behind me and whispered into my ear: 'See, the sangoma was right. It all worked out.'

Had it really worked out? Even after all that relentless digging and questioning and talking, I have to admit I still cannot say for sure who or what killed the rain queen. I can present a fascinating story of love, lust, power and betrayal. Somewhere within that drama a young woman died. But quite how remains inconclusive, to me at least.

As dusk fell, the drums were taken out into the *kgoro* and placed near the pole to which the cow was tethered. The cow had been taken off somewhere, still alive, we were assured. She would be used again next year.

There were three drums now and their beat was louder, with a deep, sombre echo. The dance became increasingly complex. First there was the swoop and clap into the centre. Then everyone fell onto their haunches, clapped and bowed their heads in silence for a few seconds. Then the drums started up again and the circle resumed its slow, hypnotic shuffle. On and on into the deepening night. Julia and I were drawn in. Still barefoot, I felt my toes squelching into the sacred cow's dung. Struggling to keep up, I noticed that the dance had changed again: everyone now had their hands raised. Someone seized my arms roughly from behind. I turned around and saw a young woman dressed like a man in baggy cotton shirt and short curly hair. I did a double take. This was what Makobo would have looked like before her fateful ascent to the throne. She thrust my arms into the air. 'Like this,' she said. After a couple more shuffles around, I dropped out of the circle and stood watching from the side. The man/woman, still absorbed in the dance, caught my eye and smiled.

Liz McGregor is a former writing fellow at WISER and currently a visiting associate at the UCT Centre for African Studies. She is the author of *Khabzela: The Life and Times of a South African*.

A Matter of Life and Death

Deborah Posel

One Sunday morning in January 2005, I received an unexpected call from Tsakane Mnisi, who headed a team of field workers working with me on a research project in rural Limpopo province. The research dealt with people's understandings and experiences of the recent proliferation of death and dying in the area – a consequence, largely, of the HIV/AIDS epidemic. Tearful and agitated, she had just arrived at the house of one of the families engaged with the research, only to find Phina – a 25-year-old woman – collapsed on the floor, barely conscious, moaning, sweating profusely, very weak, and alone.

Over a period of five months, Tsakane had been visiting Phina, to document her experience of illness and her search for treatment, in the midst of successive deaths in her family. The visits had become increasingly intimate, as Phina spoke about her uncertainty, fear and often intense physical pain; about her feelings for her family, and her vigorous will to live. Phina welcomed Tsakane's visits, eager for the opportunities to speak that the research process had opened up, in the midst of the cultural barriers and silences that structured Phina's interactions with family and friends. So Tsakane's concern for Phina was borne of a growing closeness, even if their relationship was constrained by the element of detachment that research conventions enjoin.

Tsakane wanted to get Phina to a hospital, urgently – more specifically, to the nearest hospital dispensing antiretrovirals. For she knew – as I did – that Phina had AIDS. She also knew that Phina had strenuously withheld that information from everyone else, adamant that disclosing the illness would bring shame on her and her family. As someone who shared Phina's cultural world, Tsakane was also well aware that treatment decisions – particularly in the case of someone seriously ill – were the preserve of Phina's family, not outsiders. And as researchers, both Tsakane and I were outsiders. But Tsakane was emphatic: 'It's an emergency,' she said to me, 'no-one else is here, so I want to take her to the hospital – it's a matter of life and death.'

*

It was a shock. Knowing Phina's protracted treatment history, I felt sure that she was sweating pure fear, convinced that her illness had finally felled her. Surely Tsakane was right; we had to intervene. For a brief moment I wondered whether I should drive to Limpopo there and then to support Tsakane; this wasn't going to be easy for her. But the realities of my commitments at home and at work edged that idea out of my mind. A flash of guilt, as I recognised that I was leaving Tsakane to deal with this alone, and I winced at the distance between her world and mine. Then a moment of doubt and unease: what were we getting into here?

It was a response embedded in many years of academic training: perhaps the scholarly inhibition, a preference for critique rather than action; perhaps also, the ethnographer's reflex not to impose unduly within the research setting. But in this country, at this time, it was also steeped in anxieties about race and power – jagged issues in the South African academy, still struggling to efface the apartheid world that had produced it. And all the more so in the face of the racially explosive post-apartheid politics of AIDS. The fact that rates of HIV infection were highest in the country's black population had heightened racial sensitivities. Why don't you do research on AIDS among your own people, was one of the barbed questions put to me by an angry black scholar.

As a white, middle-class, urban woman, my research was venturing into intimate and painful reaches of experience across racial, social, economic and geographical rifts. Could I justify an intervention – to get Phina onto ARVs – that would thwart the authority of Phina's family and culture, and on the basis of a reading of her illness that her family disputed, even at a moment of medical emergency? From this vantage point, it was unmistakably a transgression. Yet how could I refuse it if it promised to save a life? Wasn't this my obligation as a human being? Wouldn't it be a reiteration of the racism – and moral indifference – of the past to turn away?

So it quickly became clear: the crisis of Phina's ailing body dictated only one humane response. I felt a surge of satisfaction at the prospect of 'doing something', even if vicariously and at a distance. But the consequences of this momentary activism would not be straightforward – not for Phina, nor for Tsakane and me. We would all become entangled in the webs of secrecy and silence that enmesh the epidemic; and Tsakane and I would unwittingly become complicit in the power of AIDS stigma and the lies proliferated in its midst.

*

I had been drawn to research on HIV/AIDS despite never having worked in the field of health. In fact it wasn't the health issues that really compelled me; it was more a hunch that AIDS could lead me to the heartbeat of the post-apartheid democracy. Surely, I surmised, the way we lived with AIDS – the nation's pulse of new life in the thick of an epidemic of new death – would reveal most powerfully the forces that would shape this society.

According to the national constitution and the Truth and Reconciliation Commission – the two most powerful custodians of the new democratic ethos in the early years of post-apartheid – this was to be a society of *ubuntu*, a society formed in recognition of the humanity of the other. And it was to be ushered into being through a national commitment to truth-telling and compassion, the two critical ingredients of the glue that would bond people previously stranded across brutal racial divides, into a shared space of new-found mutuality. This was the basic logic of the TRC. There was no prospect of overcoming these breaches of the past without a full and truthful disclosure of what had happened. People who had been the victims of gross human rights violations, and whose voices and experiences of suffering had been marginalised and silenced, would be heard and acknowledged, in a forum animated by empathy and compassion. So with the truth-telling should come a propensity to forgive, and thereby to 'reconcile'. In a world mired in war and violence, it was an unashamedly hopeful, and humanist, aspiration for 'national reconciliation'.

But then came AIDS. Although incubated under apartheid, the epidemic gathered momentum as the apartheid regime expired. Along with the hopeful promises of a more dignified and compassionate life, came the menace of rampant death. And it was those who were best poised to relish the gift of freedom who were most at risk: black men and women between the ages of twenty and forty. This simultaneity of new life and new death was, in my eyes, the nub of the 'new' South Africa. How we lived with AIDS would put the hope for *ubuntu*, and the enthusiasm for truth, to its greatest test.

As it turned out, it had unsettled the presidency. During his term in office, Mandela largely ignored AIDS. Then Mbeki went to great lengths to reimagine AIDS as a more benign disease of poverty, and disputed the spectre of mass death. Viewed from the top, the 'new' South Africa seemed to be compassionate enough to forgive the transgressions and traumas of the past, but unable or unwilling to acknowledge the traumas and suffering of the present. But how did it look lower down in the society? I wanted to understand how ordinary people fashioned their lives in the thick of AIDS, how it shaped their efforts to love and care, how it challenged their powers to speak the truth. Little did I realise, at the outset of the research, how much it would challenge my own commitment to the truth and my own efforts to care.

*

Soon after Phina's hospitalisation, I made the trip up north to see how the research was progressing. Mercy, an associate of the project, met me at Nelspruit airport. Wearing a smart leather jacket, and driving her nearly new silver Jetta, Mercy was warmly confident and slipped comfortably into the role of local guide. As we drove the long haul through Mpumulanga and then into Limpopo to the sites of the research, the conversation was animated. I was struck by how much change democracy had delivered. This was not the imagery of homogeneous hardship – the uniformity of the mud huts, the barefooted and sparsely clad children, and the adults wearing the signs of a life of arduous manual labour – that rural South Africa had conjured up under apartheid. Now, as Mercy explained to me, there was much variation in the lifestyles and aspirations of black people in the countryside. People were on the move and on the make; they had new maps, new destinations. This had produced a far more stratified and fragmented world, with little resemblance to outmoded, nostalgic, versions of cohesive rural life. And the boundary between urban and rural geographies and ways of life was even more porous than it had been in the past.

We passed clusters of large brick houses – four bedrooms, two bathrooms, Mercy told me with vicarious pride, homes owned mainly by government officials, businesspeople, teachers and nurses, the core of the local elite. Several kilometres on, interspersed amidst plots with mud huts, mangy animals and teetering out-buildings, was a profusion of more modest brick homes, many with cars parked alongside and small plots of mealies planted nearby. We caught a glimpse of a domestic worker in uniform sweeping a veranda – mimicking the ways of white suburbia – while two cows meandered lethargically along the nearby road.

These new visual ironies of race, class and place then gave way to the more predictable iconography of poverty. First, the 'RDP houses' – the ANC government's ambi-guous offerings for 'a better life for all' – stark rows of identical homes, in unseemly proximity to each other, and preposterously small for the numbers they had to accommodate. But even these structures looked gene-rous in juxtaposition to the myriad shacks and huts that hadn't gone away, still the dominant feature of the landscape at large.

As we drove through a succession of small towns, many of them reincarnations of old villages, there were unmistakable signs of invigorated local economies: new shopping centres, with extensions under way; new homes under construction; in the midst of the formal shopping and business areas, hand-painted signs adver-tising the services of aspirant local entrepreneurs; and surprising numbers of expensive and new-looking cars, including shiny black BMWs – the undisputed icon of having made it in the 'new' South Africa. Yet alongside this, the lingering images of economic marginality: the children who ought to be at school, scraping through rubbish bins on the roadsides; thin and grim-looking women with large loads on their heads, walking the long hauls from their homes to sell their meagre vegetables; men sitting idly outside sparse huts.

I asked Mercy about life in these parts, for these people and for herself, after 1994. 'Things are good for me,' she responded, smiling. She and her husband, a headmaster, were happy owners of a large four-bedroom home in a small Limpopo town, with two bathrooms and three garages for the three cars they owned. In addition to her full-time administrative job, Mercy ran a lucrative business hiring out portable toilets – much in demand in these times of funerals aplenty, and she could generate a profit of R4 000 in one weekend. Then she sighed, as she told of the anxiety that accompanied her new-found prosperity. 'There are a lot of people here with no jobs, a lot, and crime is getting worse. There didn't used to be so much crime in these places, and there is so much rape; it makes me scared. The countryside isn't safe any more.'

The subject of crime elicited a wry smile from Mercy, as it led her into a story about an affluent elderly couple in her area, who had lived for many years in a large double-storey house with their children. After all the children had left home, the couple was determined not to leave the house, despite having grown too frail to use the stairs up to the second storey. So they confined themselves to the ground floor. But after a while, there were strange noises coming from upstairs. At first they imagined it was their hearing at fault, but when eventually they called the police, they discovered a ladder from the outside garden up to an upstairs window, and a stash of stolen goods in the upstairs rooms. 'Tsotsis were living upstairs; the old people were lucky that the tsotsis did not harm them.'

'Does that surprise you?' I asked.

'These days, yes, but you don't shoot the goose that lays the golden egg.' As she mused about the ways of the tsotsis, I was struck by her parable of community – an edgy and canny cohabitation, stuck together in the unsettling interplay of goodwill and menace. A different version of mutuality from the TRC's.

Then I asked Mercy about AIDS. I knew I was taking a chance. This was our first opportunity to talk at length, and I risked being impolite by launching precipitately into a subject not freely spoken about in these parts. She paused, thoughtfully. Perhaps because she was familiar with the research project, she felt free – or under pressure – to respond. 'It's the problem of the youth,' she ventured, and then stopped. I waited for her to continue. 'They have too much sex; they lack discipline.'

'But didn't your generation also have a lot of sex?' I asked, remembering many interviews in which men and women had scoffed at the idea that sexual infidelities were anything new.

'Yes, but now it's dangerous. Young people know that, but I don't think they care.'

We got stuck for a while behind a heavily laden truck, labouring up a long hill. An impatient male driver in a flashy car sped out from behind us and overtook both vehicles on the blind rise, prompting a brief sisterly exchange about men and speed. Mercy laughed, 'Now they drive like they do in Johannesburg.'

Risky masculinities brought the conversation back to AIDS. I asked her why she thought young people didn't care about the risk of AIDS. She said she didn't know, and fell silent again. I volunteered some of the comments made by young men and women during focus group discussions. AIDS is our destiny, one young man had said; 'We tell ourselves that if AIDS exists, then it means we will be infected, therefore we do not take precautions. We do as we wish. I practise sex like nobody's business and I feel proud of myself.' Others had agreed, adding that it was a fate determined by the country's liberation.

'This freedom is the key to our deaths.'

'We have the freedom to be delinquent.'

During these conversations, I had been struck by the ambivalences in their depictions of the post-apartheid moment: bursting with life – rights, freedoms, opportunities, hopes and ambitions – and riddled with death. Mercy listened intently, but chose not to comment.

*

Tsakane and I met over lunch; I wanted to know the details of Phina's hospital visit and its aftermath. As we sat down and started talking, Tsakane seemed relaxed; clearly the emotional rigours of recent weeks hadn't dented her spirit. Single mother in her mid-thirties and sole provider for her children, Tsakane wore her responsibilities lightly, with an air of youthful calm. She cut an appealing, if unimposing, figure. Obviously someone who paid careful attention to her appearance, she was fashionably dressed, even if in the modest small-town version of urban trends, with her cellphone – ubiquitous signifier of aspirant social mobility – always visible.

Tsakane relayed her struggle to get Phina's thin, wasting body to the car, their 'desperately fast' drive to the hospital, and the long and agonising wait to be seen by the first available doctor. As they sat it out, Phina had laid her head in Tsakane's lap, moaning softly, while Tsakane tried to contain her fear that Phina's life was about to expire. 'When the nurse finally came for her,' Tsakane said, her face tensing, 'I wasn't sure that I would see her again.' But three days later, she received a call from the hospital to fetch Phina, and took her back to her house, ARVs in hand. Phina's gratitude to Tsakane was effusive: 'You are the only one I can talk to; I owe you my life.'

I asked Tsakane how she felt about Phina's deepening dependency on her. 'It's fine, she needs me,' she replied, swiftly and forcefully. As the conversation progressed, I sensed her relish for the mix of altruism and power that the research project was producing for her. It resonated well with her sense of who she was, and what she wanted for herself – a person of influence and standing; someone who would offer support to others in the community and be respected and admired for it; someone who would shape the lives of others. For a young single mother of humble beginnings, living in a community fiercely defensive of old habits of male authority, it was a bold aspiration. Tsakane had told me before that South Africa's new democracy allowed a black person to 'be somebody', to come into her own. The AIDS epidemic had provided her with the space to fashion her life, I thought to myself. A space to be both caring and ambitious. Several people participating in focus group discussions had spoken out passionately about how 'disgusting' AIDS was, a sign of 'not behaving well', of moral dissolution; how parents dreaded the day that one of their children was sullied by this 'shameful' disease, and if this occurred, how fiercely they guarded the family secret to prevent outsiders 'gossiping' about their failures as parents. Offering to listen, care and support, when so many others were fearful, indifferent or hostile, required unusual commitment and compassion; it also created a sphere of recognition and authority. Many people would become indebted to her.

I asked Tsakane how Phina had felt about taking the ARVs. Phina had tried out so many different treatment regimes during her long quest for health, I wondered how she felt now about this dramatic shift to ARVs, and the responsibility of having to commit to them for the rest of her life. Tsakane didn't know. She had tried, she said, to engage Phina in talk about taking these new pills – a medicine that was still widely unknown and inaccessible in her community. But Phina had resisted, deflecting the questions into a looser conversation about her close shave with death – of which she was fully aware – and her new-found health. I asked Tsakane how she interpreted Phina's evasiveness; she said she wasn't sure, but agreed that it might have reflected some underlying resistance to the treatment on Phina's part, despite owing her life to it.

*

A few years younger than Tsakane, Phina struck a less stylish pose, with none of the confidence of the new rural consumers. Friendly in a shy sort of way, and dressed in a well-worn skirt and faded shirt, with a vivid scarf covering her head, her posture evoked more of the diffidence, deference and inscrutability that I had associated with rural black women in the past. Her slight frame and youthful demeanour gave few outward clues of the burdens of sickness and death that she carried. Only the frequent sighs and exclamations that punctuated her conversation emitted a sense of a woman under pressure. Otherwise, her bearing conformed very much to the communal norm, of carrying emotional stress and pain internally, with the dignity of silence.

If Tsakane's life had been invigorated by the energies of South Africa's youthful democracy, Phina's had been shackled by the persistent poverty and rampant death that were equally indicative of these times. Phina remembered a more prosperous family life during her childhood when both her parents were alive, but her lot was more austere now. One solace, and source of stability, was the solid, four-roomed brick house that was left to Phina and her siblings after their mother's death. She shared it with her five-year-old daughter, younger brother Caiphus, sister Thembi and Thembi's baby daughter. Caiphus's wife, and their late brother's wife, had lived with them intermittently. The household was relatively poor, even by rural standards. The house was stark and virtually empty, with little furnishing to soften the grey concrete floors, and Tsakane often noticed that there was almost no food to be had. With

Phina unable to work as a result of her lingering illness, Caiphus's paltry salary had been stretched thin, particularly in the midst of interminable medical expenses – whether it be for traditional treatments, clinic fees, or transport to one or other healer. More recently, Phina had begun receiving a childcare grant, which made a modest contribution to the family income.

Theirs had been a cohesive and supportive family for much of Phina's life, and the impact of accelerated illness had been profound. In the space of eighteen months, the siblings had lost their mother, older brother (one year after their mother's death) and older sister (a few months later). Verbal autopsies suggested that at least two of these deaths were AIDS-related; the family's versions were insistently different. Phina also lost the father of her child – a death that she did not attribute to AIDS, although she described many symptoms in common with her own.

Phina's saga of her own relentless sickness began when her mother was still alive. The earliest symptoms were episodes of diarrhoea and vomiting. Taking her mother's advice, her first port of call was the local Zion Christian Church (ZCC), to take the tea that the ZCC's healers routinely dispense to 'cleanse the stomach'. This tea is the preferred medication for strict followers of the ZCC, whose hopes for health are vested largely in the intense spectacle of prayer, enacted by the groups of worshippers who dance and sing for hours on end. Phina's attitude, however, was more plural. After several portions of the ZCC remedy, over a period of many months, she developed swellings on her feet that became very painful, and a bad cough set in. At this point, she took herself off to the local clinic, where she was given some medicine – without any suggestion of an HIV test. She felt better for a while, but then the pain resumed. She went back to the clinic, for a repeat of the medication – but again, after a temporary reprieve, the pain returned. After several such visits, the clinic sister eventually suggested that she take an HIV test. 'It was tough,' Phina said, 'but I thought, well, let me give it a try.'

This was in 2003. The test came back positive. 'It was as if my life was falling apart; the truth is, I didn't believe it. I continued to live like normal but my heart was painful.' It was a struggle that she bore alone; Phina chose not to tell anyone about the HIV.

Shortly after the test, Phina became very ill, and her family took her to one of the provincial hospitals, where another blood test was done. 'But they didn't tell me I was HIV-positive; they only said I had TB. So I clung to TB.' This did not dispel the dread of the HIV, but it gave her a palatable version of her illness to share with her family.

The illness continued, on and off. Phina's mother, her own health rapidly deteriorating, took Phina back to the ZCC for the tea. 'I felt better and went back to work,' Phina said. Episodes of weakness and pain recurred, however. Phina's siblings now informed her that her ancestors were angry, and that she should seek help from a sangoma in the area. Phina did not contest the diagnosis; 'If brother Caiphus can know that Phina has AIDS, it will destroy him; it is better that he does not find out.' Referring to her family at large, she was equally adamant: 'I would not tell them; I will die without telling them what is killing me.' So Phina consulted a local sangoma. The experience was initially reassuring, but ultimately unsatisfying. Despite a feeling of well-being in the immediate aftermath of the consultation, her illness did not abate, and Phina began to feel a mounting sense of despair that she would never be well again.

Throughout this period, Phina continued having sex with two men – one, a married man with whom she had a fairly discreet relationship; the other, the father of her child and her more serious emotional attachment. She told neither man about the HIV and did not press for the use of condoms – in the case of the father of her child, because 'I wouldn't risk losing him'. So 'we lived like everything was okay'. But both men became seriously ill, and the father of her child subsequently died. Phina remains adamant that neither was afflicted with AIDS despite recognising many of her symptoms in theirs. With similar ambivalence – of seeing and not seeing AIDS, knowing and not knowing about AIDS – Phina did not want to have her child tested for HIV. 'I am afraid to do that,' she told Tsakane. 'I just hope that she is healthy.'

By late 2004, Phina's mother had died, along with her older brother and sister. The financial rigours of losing two of the family's breadwinners compounded the grief. There were new familial stresses too, as Phina's relationships with her sisters-in-law grew increasingly conflictual. 'Life was very difficult,' she recalls, and her own health began to deteriorate rapidly. Her younger brother Caiphus, who had himself been suffering intermittent bouts of sickness, decided that as the eldest surviving male in the household, he ought to intervene. Phina was taken back to the hospital and admitted for two days, but the experience was distressing for her as well as her brother. Unable to eat and rapidly losing weight, Phina was informed by the hospital staff that they could do nothing for her, and she was discharged.

Alarmed, Caiphus decided to call for help within the wider extended family. His late mother's brother, living hundreds of miles away in Johannesburg, advised that Phina be sent to a healer he had heard about in a near-by village. Phina protested despairingly to Caiphus that 'she was very tired of going up and down with healers, so she had better stay and die here at home'. He found her resistance to treatment troubling, and turned once again to his uncle, who then decided to drive up from Johannesburg to take charge of the situation in person.

Fond and respectful of her uncle, Phina then relented, and she spent two weeks in the homestead of the healer whom he had selected. This healer had trained as a sangoma and also served as a bishop in the African Zionist Church, so he offered a combination of traditional and faith-healing methods. Caiphus and his uncle visited Phina at the healer's home several times. During their first visit, they noted that she had difficulty eating, and could barely swallow the mixture that the healer had made for her. But by the next visit, a few days later, they found her somewhat recovered, 'able to sit and talk to us fluently, able to eat food on her own, though she was eating very little food.' And she continued to take 'the medicine'. By the beginning of her second week there, Caiphus reckoned that 'although she was not that much strong, we could see that she is going to be healed. She became better and better and it went on like that until she finally came home.'

After the dispiriting experience of Phina's hospitalisation, Caiphus felt relieved that her condition was not hopeless after all. His conviction was short-lived, however, as Phina's illness returned. Phina now asked to be taken back to the hospital – a request that surprised Caiphus, since her recent encounters with the health service had been so alienating. But he obliged, reluctantly, and Phina was duly admitted. Only to be discharged two days later. What worried Caiphus most about this episode in hospital was Phina's inability to eat there, as compared with the healthier appetite she had developed while staying with the healer – a powerful sign, for Caiphus, of her greater responsiveness to the healer's care. So, on her return from the hospital, he took Phina back to the same healer.

A few days later, she called for Caiphus to take her back home, feeling stronger – so much so that Caiphus felt able to leave her and go off to work in a nearby town. This was early January 2005, and Phina was hopeful that the new year would give her a new lease on life. But the improvement was short-lived, and Phina's condition plummeted almost immediately after Caiphus left. As Phina became desperately ill, it was fortuitous that Tsakane decided to pay her a surprise visit one Sunday morning, and found her in a state of collapse, on the floor. This was the day that Tsakane took Phina to hospital for the ARVs that would save her life. After years of increasingly debilitating pain and despair, punctuated with bouts of treatment that offered fickle promises of recovery, Phina would now experience the most dramatic and enduring turnaround in her condition. She would gain weight; her skin would be restored to its youthful smoothness; she would recover the energy to move about, laugh and converse; and she would feel sufficiently revived to return to her job at a local store. Her body – her life – would be resurrected.

There was one more hurdle, however, a reminder of how Phina's renewed lease on life was bound up with the life of the research project. In July, I decided to make a trip to Limpopo, to see how Phina was doing. Tsakane had told me how wonderfully Phina had responded to the ARVs; I wanted to see her revival for myself. Tsakane and I arrived at Phina's house on a wintry Sunday morning, expecting to find her in exuberant health. She was sitting outside in a rickety chair, placed hopefully in a thin ray of warm sun. As the car drove into the property, Phina smiled and waved a greeting, and then struggled to walk towards us. She was listless and sweating, and her eyes seemed glazed. After the familiar pleasantries, Phina informed us that for the past three months she had not taken any ARV medication. During her March visit to the hospital that Tsakane had taken her to in January, which was relatively close to Phina's village, the staff had summarily refused to treat her there and instructed her to travel to another hospital, much further away. Apparently there had been some bureaucratic change of plan, but there was little effort to communicate it and Phina couldn't fathom the reason for the shift. Nor could she afford the R50 taxi fare, and therefore had had no option but to stop the treatment.

Once again, our obligation seemed clear. I asked

Tsakane to use the car at the disposal of the research project to take Phina to the more remote hospital the next day, wait with her there until she had been attended to, and then drive her back home (predictably a full day's undertaking). And since then, it has been Tsakane who has driven Phina to get her ARVs each and every month. The pity of it is that the car could carry two more passengers; but Tsakane has not been able to seek out others in Phina's vicinity who were taking ARVs – a sign of the silence shrouding the epidemic, rather than any lack of need for treatment.

*

At this point in the story, Caiphus' version of what had happened to Phina diverges starkly from Phina's. He attributes her extraordinary recovery to the special powers of the healer. What he doesn't know is that it was shortly after Phina's last return from the healer's homestead that Tsakane had chanced upon her, seriously ill and barely conscious. Nor does he know about the hospital visit and the ARVs that Phina was given.

Phina was one of the fortunate patients whose bodies respond readily to ARVs with no complications or side-effects. A beneficiary of the modest roll-out of ARVs through the public sector in Limpopo province, she no longer has to struggle with recurrent bouts of illness, and as her family and community see her, is fully recovered. That she has been taking ARV medication has remained a secret. And despite the fact that she knows full well that these pills rescued her from imminent death, and has felt how her health dips precipitously when she stops taking them, Phina continues to resist efforts to talk about them – as if still somehow in denial of her life-long dependency on this regime of treatment.

*

Phina's uncle soon heard of her amazing recovery, which he attributed – understandably – to the healing skills of his preferred healer. He had paid in the region of R2 500 for the treatment, but wanted further to demonstrate his gratitude to the man. So, when the healer asked him to sponsor a large party for the community to celebrate Phina's newfound health, the uncle was happy to oblige.

I heard about the healer's request during one of my visits to the area. The immediacy of being there – spending time in the homes of families burdened by the pain of many deaths, witnessing the poverty, the ubiquitous illness, and the tenuous dignity with which people struggled to keep going – heightened my horror at the news. I was uncomfortable at the prospect of being complicit in such a deception. The country was in the throes of intense political argument about appropriate treatment for HIV/AIDS, with the Minister of Health openly sceptical about the efficacy of ARVs and seeming to promote scientifically untested alternative remedies for AIDS. I didn't pretend to be neutral, and shared the frustration of AIDS activists at the paucity of effective political leadership on the subject of treatment, and the ensuing uncertainty and confusion in many communities living in the midst of AIDS. So did I not have an obligation to the truth? There are many instances in which the idea of a single truth is implausible, as different cultural forms fashion their own. But this was not one of those cases: we knew incontrovertibly, as did Phina, that it was the ARVs rather than the healer that had made her well. Yet Phina had spoken to us on condition that we respected her refusal to disclose that she had AIDS and was using ARVs. Her dignity, then, was at stake. Did our obligation to her override the obligation to expose a lie? And what about any obligations to the wider community? But if we betrayed Phina's trust, what would the ripple effect be within other households party to the research? Would we forfeit their trust too?

In other areas of the country, we might have been able to turn to NGOs or community leaders who had taken a prominent stand on AIDS, for advice and help. But not in these parts. Nor had government-initiated programmes to educate healers about AIDS and draw them in to partnerships with the district health services taken root here. So we had to deal with the dilemma on our own.

As I struggled to come up with a coherent position, I had long talks with Tsakane about her views. She was unusually hesitant: 'Whatever we do, it is risky.' Intensely uneasy about interfering with Phina's family and breaching her trust, Tsakane was just as uncomfortable about being party to what she considered an outright lie. She also understood its powers. The research project had by then revealed the extent to which local communities relied on the services of healers, as they had done ever since they could remember, and the veneration of the healers in spite of mixed experiences in their care. We also knew about people's frustrations with, and suspicions of, the local health services, to the point that many regarded the hospitals as the source of deadly infection. And the acceleration of death in the area prompted feelings of uncertainty and alarm, even despair. In this milieu, news about a miraculous cure could ignite fires of hope that would spread swiftly and furiously. 'It would be better if we could stop it,' she sighed, her voice raised as if asking a question as much as taking a position.

For Tsakane, the difficulties of this moment were also embedded in deeper challenges that characterised her position as a field worker on the project. As a member of the local community, she had experienced the shame of AIDS up close. During the previous year, her own sister had died of AIDS, but her family had never said as much, retreating into the cultural norms that discourage open conversation about death – the more so in the case of a young person whose illness had closely resembled the dreaded 'disease of today'. And Tsakane had found the silence difficult to resist. 'It's hard to speak out, the silence on AIDS is powerful; I feel it too. I don't talk openly about AIDS,' she had told me. She had been drawn to the research project, she said, because she hoped it would 'help people talk openly about their feelings or about issues regarding AIDS or regarding death'. As the project progressed, she had also grown increasingly impatient with local versions of what AIDS was – a medical conspiracy, or a result of witchcraft, or a symptom of *tindzhaka* (a traditional illness caused by a breach of cultural norms regulating sex in the aftermath of a family death). Now persuaded by the science of AIDS, she felt a personal mission, 'to tell my community the truth about AIDS.' So it was with some reluctance that she conceded that her responsibilities as a field worker prioritised insightful questioning, acute observation, and above all, empathic listening. This dualism had troubled her relationship with Phina on several occasions already, when the pressure to intervene in Phina's life had felt almost irresistible. For example, when Phina told Tsakane that she had continued having unprotected sex with a variety of men despite knowing her HIV status, Tsakane told me how this had enraged her: 'I wanted to shout at her.'

My position on the healer's proposed party grew more uncertain and confused. I had a long argument with my husband, a doctor, for whom the choice was straightforward: there was only one ethically defensible option, he insisted, which was to 'tell the uncle, if Phina won't do it herself, or tell the healer'. He was frustrated at my limp indecision. I was feeling more wary about weighing in now, than I had been when Tsakane had found Phina in a heap on the floor, and could not recreate the clarity of that first decision. There was no immediate risk of death, even if claims to specious healing powers would likely endanger many lives. But how much of this was my responsibility? And then there was the question of race. I argued with myself: which was the more racially paternalist response, to leave Phina and her community to a spectacle of lies, or to act in the name of truth, breaching Phina's trust and overriding her dignity as someone who could make her own decisions and take responsibility for their consequences? Had I capitulated to the black authenticity argument, to stay out of things I didn't and couldn't fully understand? Was it a racial issue in fact? Would I – should I – have reacted any differently if Phina had been a white woman?

In the end, my judgment was more a product of my failure to resolve these questions than any coherent or definitive reasoning. So it was ultimately Tsakane – black woman, confidante, close to Phina's world and culture – who felt a stronger urge to forestall the healer's celebration than I – white, middle-class, academic stranger, wary of racial misdemeanours.

Tsakane and I agreed that what we should do was to try to persuade Phina into a change of heart. So, during several conversations with Phina about the proposed celebration, Tsakane made her own views known. Phina's thinking, however, did not shift. Her uncle, she said, had demonstrated his firm commitment to her and her family, investing a large sum of money in her treatment. By now, the truth had become altogether too dangerous. To suddenly disclose that she had had AIDS all along would, she felt, undermine her family's trust. 'Everyone in the family believes I have been helped by the healer; that is why they paid him well.' Admitting that she had been taking ARVs would make a mockery of her uncle, her family and the healer – a profoundly disrespectful act, she maintained, to all the people close to her and to whom she felt deeply grateful. She worried too, that it would provoke their anger. AIDS had already taken so much from her, and what was left was fragile. Caiphus's wife had recently left the house 'for fear of death'. Phina feared that abandoning her secret would finally rip the family apart. She made

Tsakane promise faithfully, once again, that she would not betray Phina's trust.

So the event went ahead. On a dry and dusty morning in late August, a crowd assembled at the healer's homestead, to hear him thank his ancestors for giving him the power to cure Phina's affliction. He did not name it, but described it as a deadly assault on the body and the community. AIDS was never mentioned, yet in recounting the ways of the illness and how it sabotaged Phina's health, it must have been abundantly clear to the people gathered there that these were the familiar symptoms of the dreaded disease that was cutting a swathe through their social body. As they mingled and talked over a lunch of pap and beef, courtesy of Phina's uncle, the conversation must have applauded the miracle of having discovered someone who could vanquish the enemy in their midst.

Tsakane interviewed the healer after the event. He told her that he had been sure that Phina had AIDS, because he could recognise her symptoms. 'She was too thin and she was coughing; her feet were swollen, she lost hair, with her skin peeling.' Tsakane had asked him his views about what causes AIDS. 'It is caused by the Western influence on black people's lifestyles,' he replied. 'People are using condoms thinking that they prevent AIDS infections whereas the condoms contain worms that cause infections on a male private part, and the male passes the infections on to a woman during sexual intercourse. Young people are still going to die in large numbers because they are the ones who use condoms.' He vowed to do whatever he could to save them from this error.

If the healer could deduce that Phina had AIDS, he did not know about the ARVs – and therefore, in good faith, believed that Phina's dramatic recovery proved that he had the power to cure AIDS. And the crowd bore witness to the extraordinary gift of life he had given Phina. A vital, exuberant body, in place of one that had been wasting away, corroded by swellings and sores, was incontrovertible evidence of his success.

*

Phina's health has not deserted her and she continues to take her ARVs regularly. Her sister Thembi however, has lost a lot of weight and takes ill with worrying regularity. Her symptoms resemble her sister's at an earlier stage of her illness. She also cries a lot, which upsets Tsakane. 'Maybe it's all that anger that is making her emotionally unwell,' Tsakane suggests, as we talk about it. Thembi had her first child when she was fourteen, in the same year that she lost her mother.

Tsakane has asked Phina if she would consider talking to Thembi about HIV/AIDS, and advising her to have herself tested for HIV. But Phina has refused, frightened by the prospect that this conversation might impel her to confess her HIV status to Thembi.

Phina's secret might not be as tight as she thinks, or hopes. When Phina once reprimanded Thembi for her many sexual flings, Thembi's response was taunting: 'Why should I? You did the same, and now you have AIDS.' Phina did not reply; the conversation died, never to be resuscitated. And Phina has ceased trying to intervene in her sister's lifestyle and health – although she confesses to Tsakane that she worries about Thembi's future.

As Tsakane tells me this, the jagged edges of the research resurface. I see Phina's predicament; the research has helped me to understand and respect her spaces of choice, as well as the factors that constrain these choices. But I can't quell a rising frustration at the power of stigma in her world. There are hopeful signs of a more honest and open acceptance of the realities of AIDS in communities elsewhere in the country, where organisations such as Médecins Sans Frontières and the Treatment Action Campaign have galvanised local efforts to tackle the epidemic in their midst. Some of these initiatives – fired by the missionary zeal of extraordinarily committed doctors, nurses and AIDS activists – have achieved a measure of communal openness to disclosure and treatment, which has made it easier for individuals to breach the silence so strongly associated with the epidemic. But in Phina's community, there are still relatively few people on ARV treatment, and she has no social links with others who are prepared to acknowledge being HIV-positive or sick with AIDS. So she still lives with her illness in isolation and silence, allowing the force of shame to shackle her.

I am also struck by the tragic irony of Phina's situation. ARVs gave her back her life, as she well knows; but she won't reveal that because she fears it will kill her family – a caring, supportive family that Phina is desperate not to offend. Yet Phina's secret is now beginning to strangle the very vestiges of family that she craves. Unable to speak to Thembi, Phina seems resigned to Thembi's worsening illness, perhaps even her death.

I wonder about our responsibilities, if any, to Thembi, as her place in her family grows increasingly tenuous. She is sexually reckless – wilfully so – and is absent from the house for long periods, without informing her siblings where she is and abandoning her child to Phina's care. This has made her relationships with her siblings, particularly Caiphus, intensely conflictual, to the point that Caiphus feels he can no longer communicate effectively with her. So who will take care of Thembi?

Tsakane and I talk it through. We have spent relatively little time with Thembi, and she seems more remote to me than Phina. From a distance, she cuts a defiant and brittle figure; I imagine it will be hard to reach her. Tsakane expresses her disappointment with Phina's will to secrecy, and feels unable to turn a blind eye to Thembi's situation. So do I, but I still feel an obligation to Phina. Tsakane agrees; she recently committed herself, once again, to honouring Phina's secret. We decide, therefore, that Tsakane should try to broach the subject of AIDS with Thembi in general, impersonal terms. So she has resolved to bring AIDS booklets available at a local clinic to Thembi, in the hope that these might encourage her to take an HIV test. But we know that this is improbable. Having witnessed the wondrous life that was revived in her sister's deathly body at the hands of the now renowned healer, why would Thembi look elsewhere for the restoration of her ailing health?

Deborah Posel is the director of WISER. She is the author of *The Making of Apartheid 1948-1961: Conflict and Compromise* and coeditor, most recently, of *Commissioning the Past: Understanding South Africa's Truth and Reconciliation Commission.*

Moving In, Moving Out

Graeme Reid

Some people see me as a gay man, a researcher from Johannesburg. But if you hear the *ladies* talking about me you will be left with a different impression. The *ladies* call me Thembi, 'the country girl with a city style'. I know that this name, Thembi, shows that I am included amongst the coterie of *ladies*. It means that I have made that subtle shift from outsider to almost-insider. 'Insider' in this case means being part of a group of gays living in the township of Wesselton in Ermelo, Mpumalanga. Gays in this community refer to each other as *ladies*, their boyfriends as *gents*. They tell me that *ladies* are gay and *gents* are straight. It is in this arena of *ladies* and *gents* that my epithet has evolved. It started with 'country girl'. It started while I was walking through the veld near Platrand, a farming district not far from Standerton in Mpumalanga.

I am walking through the veld with Bhuti. (If I am 'country girl', then Bhuti is 'key informant'.) I want to meet Nhlanhla, whom Bhuti calls his 'daughter in gay life'. Bhuti told me that when Nhlanhla first came to him as a young gay, still in high school, confused and bewildered, Bhuti took him under his wing. He showed

77

Nhlanhla the ropes. He offered him advice. He encouraged him to be respectable and discouraged him from loud company and too many boyfriends.

Nhlanhla lives on a farm with his parents. His mother does domestic work in the farmhouse while his father drives tractors. Nhlanhla is a healer. He works with bones and herbs. Although he has been here before, Bhuti can't quite remember which cluster of mud-and-thatch huts is home to Nhlanhla. As we walk, the veld gives way to marshland. There is no way around it. To get to the huts we must walk through the mud. Bhuti uses thumb and forefinger to hitch his trouser legs out of mud's way, gingerly trying to step on dry tufts of grass. I am wearing boots and jeans and squelch happily through the mud. This is when Bhuti first calls me 'country girl', in an ironic blend of admiration and disapproval.

The 'city style' suffix comes later. 'What is "city" about me?' I ask the *ladies*. Evidently it has something to do with my driving. I am overconfident in small towns, it seems, and too cautious in the countryside. They tell me that I drive around country towns as if I am in rush-hour traffic. I only pause at stop signs. I take short cuts. I do U-turns on the main street. And yet I am anxious about overtaking on country roads. My accoutrements also denote 'city' – sunglasses, cellphone and watch. Or rather it is the labels, not just the things – Ray-Bans, Motorola and Swatch are 'city style'. My technologies are also 'city' – laptop, digital audio recorder and digital camera. I recognise that 'city style' is also a reminder, a caution, a signal of difference. I don't quite belong here. I will leave again. I will move back to the city. But I can be a country girl, at least for a while.

I don't particularly want to be a girl anything, country or city, but I am touched by my label. I am going to be working and living amongst the *ladies* and so I am grateful to be accepted as one. It is important to be inside – my research requires it. And, as I am to discover during the months of toing and froing between city and countryside, Thembi needs it. As a *lady* amongst other *ladies*, I know that she will be protected. But she will also be vulnerable. You can't have it both ways. So I (or Thembi) take my cue from other, more experienced, *ladies* and move into the 'gay palace' which consists of rented rooms, called flats, behind a row of shops in Wesselton.

I am bemused to learn that my black landlords are called *Baas* and *Missus*. I have never used these terms to address anyone before and, in my white South African persona, I feel very uncomfortable when addressed, as one inevitably is, as *Baas*. I try to discourage people from doing so. And yet here I am paying my rent and saying 'hello *Baas*' and 'hello *Missus*'. The rent is R300 a month. Missus and Baas are a young, hard-working couple. They manage the rooms and the shops, they run a general store and they also own a funeral parlour. The sign on the side of their shop reads: *Fish and Chips and General Dealer*. The sign is sponsored by Coca-Cola and bears the ubiquitous logo. The shop sells all the basics – including soap, tinned fish, Vaseline, tea, sugar, biscuits and large plastic bags filled with orange crisps popular with shebeen proprietors. Chips cook perpetually in a large vat of recycled oil. These are popular as a takeaway accompanied by *atchar* sold in small opaque plastic containers with bright red lids. When it rains, collapsed cardboard boxes keep some of the mud and rain off the untreated cement floor. A metal grille separates the customers from Missus and Baas. There was a rumour that the funeral parlour was going to be housed in the row of shops in front of my rooms. I am immensely relieved when it is built elsewhere. The sign on the funeral parlour reads: '*Just sit and relax, we will do the rest.*'

The shops and rooms are in a new part of the township. This area started as a spillover from the existing township. It began with handmade houses built from corrugated iron on wooden frames. Then basic services came – water and electricity. Houses made from breeze block or brick sprang up between the corrugated iron. The roads follow haphazard routes, weaving between houses, following contours that cause erosion so that when it rains the few cars that use them have to weave around deep craters. Here and there gullies are filled with stones and dry grass so that minibus taxis, the only means of public transport in these parts, can pass.

The rooms are rudimentary, but from my bedroom I have a view over the township to the fields and hills beyond. The floors are uneven, but they are built well off the ground, so that when there is a downpour and the dusty yard is turned into mud and slush, at least these rooms stay dry – more or less. Rain still creeps in under the roof, leaving grey streaks on the walls. This is one of the reasons that Bhuti, now my neighbour, moved here in the first place. His previous rooms flooded every time there was a storm.

The other problem for Bhuti was the seemingly endless series of break-ins at his previous place. I used to stay with him, sharing his room and his bed, usually with three or four other *ladies* – some on his bed, others on a thin foam mattress on the floor. I don't like sharing in the best of circumstances but this is how things are done and it did not feel right to be in a guest house, remote, removed. But my visits invariably coincided with a burglary – sometimes while I was there, sometimes shortly after I left. We thought that it must have something to do with my presence. I had a car, after all, and obviously had resources. One night, in Bhuti's bed, I woke up from a vivid dream. Someone was climbing though his window, carrying a knife. It took me a while to realise that it was only a dream. I decided then that I did not want to stay there any more. And shortly thereafter, when Bhuti saw armed men at the shebeen next door, he too decided that it was time to move. The security here is better – Baas makes a point of driving by late at night or in the early hours of the morning to check up on things, the grounds are fenced and someone always stays in the old caravan, a rickety structure resting on bricks, near the gate.

I move into flat number four, my two rooms. The number, in ornate gold lettering, is one of the very few gestures towards an aesthetic that is not purely functional. Three *ladies* help me move in. They are youngsters, late teenagers, early twenties. Manti, Tsepo and S'thembeli. They are all close to Bhuti. At 34, Bhuti plays the role of mentor to many younger gays. In this capacity he is known as 'aunty'. Although I know him, Manti introduces himself to me in a camp drawl: 'Hi, I am Manti, exotic dancer and hooker.' Bhuti jokes with him that he is getting plump and they argue about whether *gents* go for a svelte or more rounded look. Manti dresses fashionably, and designs his own clothes. Tsepo is at the local technical college and tonight there will be something of a celebration because in the morning he will have his picture taken for the local newspaper, the *Highveld Advertiser*. He has achieved five distinctions. Tsepo has modest ambitions. He would like to have a husband, a house and a car. He dreams of adopting children. S'thembeli is still in high school. He has a reputation as a skilled hair-braider, something that he learned from his sister.

With the help of these three *ladies* I sweep the rooms, hang pictures and curtains, arrange my eclectic collection of furniture and make up the bed. I have a plan. I know where everything is going – the place for my bed, couch, desk. I know where the pictures will hang. Like so many other ordinary and everyday events this is turned into a mini-drama. The game is maids and madams. It is choreographed by Manti who becomes madam and we his maids. Then I am also madam, and so it goes on. In this game, Tsepo becomes Sarah. Manti, as madam, addresses Sarah sharply and condescendingly. 'Sarah,' says Manti, 'Sarah, I don't want you drinking with my guests.'

'Sorry madam,' Tsepo joins in without a moment's hesitation, 'but the other madam opened a bottle of wine …' In the meantime they help me with my duvet cover. Sarah, the maid, reminisces how she learned to make beds when she worked in the household of a well-known mining magnate in Johannesburg. She says that she was fired for sleeping with the boss.

There was a particular advertisement on television at the time which the *ladies* found very funny. They told me about it. The advertisement showed a white maid picking up after a rich black family. The maid was taken for granted and ignored. The black madam drove past a township in her 4x4. There were only whites living in the township. There was a moment when the black driver of the vehicle stopped at a traffic light and on seeing a group of white youths, pointedly locked her door. The advertisement struck a chord, and, in sharing it with me, we laughed at our own brief flaunting of the norms.

Nathi is a hairstylist in town. He works at the Professional Hair Salon owned by Missus's mother. He attends church with Missus on Wednesday evening and Sunday morning. In fact we got these rooms because of Nathi. Missus told Nathi, Nathi told Bhuti, Bhuti told me. While I am settling in, Nathi, a slim figure at once fragile and resolute, shy and composed, pops into my room dressed in his Zionist church uniform, the one worn by women members of his congregation, and, with his characteristic gold tooth flashing in the glare of my single bare light bulb, he asks, 'Graeme, how can your husband let you come here with all your things?'

This prompts some investigative journalism. Manti transforms himself from madam to journalist, and fires questions at me from behind his microphone. 'Are you divorcing your husband?' he asks, while gesturing to the young S'thembeli to take photographs. 'A scoop!' Manti declares, 'A scoop!' This becomes a refrain in my field work. After a day of interviews, I will be asked 'Any scoops?' I am gently mocked and teased in my role as researcher. But, as Thembi, I can also eavesdrop on 'GGC', an acronym for the gay gossip column, which is a rich source of information for me and highly entertaining for Thembi.

I am very pleased to find these two small rooms. I am excited about having my own place. I have a sense that I have a lot to learn from the *ladies* and that a whole new set of experiences is about to unfold. And yet, I am soon to learn that the definition of 'my own place' is not that clear cut. I should have known from Bhuti's room with his group of sleepover guests that nothing, including space, would belong to me alone. Here in the gay palace everything is shared. For me this takes some getting used to. Minor items go astray – where is my mug? How did my mirror end up in the Wesselton Hall during a beauty pageant? It also takes a while for me to accept that people will simply wander in and out for a quick chat, to borrow this or that, for a place to sleep, to wash, to change. Things circulate, but miraculously always seem to come back. They are always somewhere to be found in one or other part of the gay palace and its environs. The mirror is back in its place, the mug was next door and when I really need peace and quiet, my rooms are my own.

Next door Bhuti is cooking the evening meal. He has a knack of turning everything into something of an occasion. Tonight it is Tsepo's academic achievements that are being celebrated. But Bhuti also takes the opportunity to remonstrate with the other *ladies* about the forthcoming beauty pageant, Miss Gay Ten Years of

Democracy. He scolds Tsepo and Manti for not planning their outfits yet. They discuss hairstyling techniques. Tsepo says that he is going to opt for a wig. He says that black hair salons will not offer eyelash perms, and he is too scared to ask at the white salon in town. Before I know it, I am drawn into various arrangements – Could I ask someone to design a poster? Will I type up the programme on my computer? Will I help to secure the hall? Can I pay the deposit? I find that the boundaries between 'participant' and 'observer' are constantly being stretched and tested. Bhuti shares his dream of opening a catering company – Tasty Buds, it will be called. Meanwhile the dinner overflows from his undersized pots, 'Life in the ghetto,' he remarks, laconically.

Later that night, when I need something from the shops, Bhuti sends S'thembeli to accompany me. Even here, he tells me, it is not safe to walk the short distance alone. There is a shebeen here, and while it is strictly controlled and the pounding music stops abruptly at 9 pm, the rule of thumb is that where there is alcohol, there is danger.

Ladies, I learn, are no strangers to violence. They are often mugged. *Ladies* are seen to be easy targets with a reputation for having money and expensive accessories.

At one of Bhuti's parties, held at his previous place before he moved to the gay palace, I was accosted by a man in his backyard. He said, 'I love you, I love you so much. Let us go and talk where no-one can see us. I know I am a black man and you are white, but just give me a chance to show you how much I love you. I want you to be my girlfriend.' Thembi was a bit taken aback,

85

having never laid eyes on him before, and had no intention of going 'where no-one could see us'. A group of *ladies* appeared from nowhere and escorted me away to a safe house nearby. They knew him and also knew that I was in danger.

I feel safe with the *ladies*. At various times, I am escorted out of danger, I am forewarned and I am physically protected. I feel safer in flat number four than I have felt with panic buttons and electric fencing in Johannesburg. But I am in strange territory, and I stand out as the only white person in the township. I am obviously a stranger and an outsider.

But strangers are not the only threat to *ladies*. Their boyfriends, *gents*, can be quite rough and aggressive. Bhuti's boyfriend visits on the day that I move in. He and Bhuti are not getting along at the moment. His boyfriend is jealous of Bhuti's wide social network and has confiscated his cellphone. Now he monitors all his calls. And Bhuti is not supposed to go anywhere without informing him first. He is friendly to me though, and unusually forthcoming. We have a short chat. Talking is not his style. He is wearing a black beret and he sits on his haunches. Bhuti slips some cash to Manti who nips out to get the *gent* a beer from the shebeen. When the quart is finished he leaves saying that he will be back for dinner, but he never arrives.

Tsepo's former boyfriend, Kagiso, also arrives at Bhuti's place for a brief visit. My arrival has caused quite a stir and people are coming to see for themselves. The last time I saw Kagiso with Tsepo, there had been a fight. Bhuti was hosting a party. Tsepo had left reluctantly when his boyfriend insisted that he should. Then Tsepo returned a short while later crying and with his shirt torn. Kagiso had beaten him. Kagiso told me later that it was the first time that he had done that: 'Honestly I never beat any person before, neither a gay nor a woman.' Kagiso has two young children. He told me that he has not decided whether he will settle down with a woman or a gay. 'I still have that homework on my mind. I'm still doing that research,' he said.

When Kagiso has left, Bhuti eases the palpable tension in the room by staging something between a talk show and a mock counselling session for Tsepo. 'How did it feel at the time? Do you think you will be able to forgive him?'

It is late by the time I get into bed on my first night in flat number four. It is July and freezing. I breathe out steam as I lie in bed under my duvet with my hot-water bottle. There is no ceiling, just the bare corrugated-iron roof. There is a plug and an overhead light bulb in each room. My bedding has absorbed the smell of smoke from coal fires. The air is thick with it and everything, it seems, is coated in a fine layer of soot. This coal has to be the opposite of the smokeless anthracite available in Johannesburg. As the evening fires are lit in winter, I think of Charles Dickens. I think of Eastern Europe in Soviet days. As I drift off to sleep I have a vague thought that surely there must be some sort of regulation, some industry standard regarding coal. I have permitted myself a luxury, an electric blanket, and it is set on high. I come to regret this before the night is out. When I wake up I find that I have run out of electricity. Bhuti estimated that my prepaid electricity would last a week. I am both annoyed and slightly ashamed that I have used it all in one night. Now I can't even make a cup of tea and must wait to buy more electrical units from the supplier in town.

There is no running water inside the rooms. There are two communal taps outside that work periodically and intermittently. There are also two outside toilets about a hundred metres away from my rooms. They both have ill-fitting metal doors, neither of which closes. When one morning both outside taps that service the gay palace once again do not produce a drop of water and the two toilets with the never-closing metal doors remain conspicuously unflushed and clogged with scraps of newspaper, I am told: 'Yes, there is no water,' an everyday fact and a common occurrence. No water – a simple fact of life. At some point it will flow again – maybe later today, maybe this evening. Who knows? Whereas I can't even think about starting my day without at least being able to wash my face, clean my teeth. My instinct is to phone someone, complain, and insist on the water being turned on. But phone whom? Complain to whom? And what result will it have? And who has airtime to make the call? I can see that resignation is more appropriate than agitation. I can get into my car and buy mineral water, sparkling or still, from a garage. As a house-warming gesture I bring two rosebushes – one for Bhuti, as my neighbour, and one for me. During the course of my stay, we will water these plants with the dirty water from bathing or washing up.

From the moment I arrive in Wesselton with my eclectic selection of furniture I of course know that I can leave at any time. And I do leave. When I leave, I also leave most of my furniture behind. I have no use for it anyway. Although I know that the name for second-hand goods around here is '*Dankie Missus*'. I take bits and pieces – things of sentimental value and that framed print of African headdresses and masks that hangs on my wall. I leave a lot behind, but I take more than enough with me. My rooms are let out to a woman who works at Game, a store recently opened in Ermelo. She will be moving in the next day. I take a different route home. The N17 is bleak with its endless line of heavy-duty trucks passing through industrialised sites and sad, shabby towns – Bethal, Leandra, Secunda. Instead I take the road to Morgenzon. It is longer and slower and there are stretches of potholed asphalt, but it is gentler, more scenic. I have left room number four behind and in doing so I am also leaving Thembi. I re-inhabit my old self. Although, as my old silver Mercedes glides along these quiet country roads heading towards Johannesburg, and now and again I must bolt and swerve at the unexpected pothole craters, I find myself thinking 'city style'.

Graeme Reid is a researcher at WISER. He is the editor, most recently, of *Sex and Politics in South Africa*.

Neighbours

Makhosazana Xaba

I wrote down my needs on a piece of paper and told my estate agent not to call me unless she had something that fitted my description exactly. I wanted a decent place my daughter and I could call home. And I wanted to do this before I turned 40 in a year's time. It was 1996.

I heard from her six months later. I went to view the house. It was semidetached, in a street lined with jacaranda trees. I promptly made an offer. 'We were the first Indians, I mean black people, to move to this street,' the occupants told me when I met them. The semidetached houses were very close to one another but with just enough space to give one a sense of privacy and of community in equal measure. Although I had not excluded the idea of semidetachment when I wrote my estate agent a brief, I wasn't very keen on it. But I had really warmed to the place. Mostly because of its spaces. Being of rural origins meant being used to large spaces. As we drove towards the area my sister said, 'I like the aura of this area. I think I'll like the house.'

I wanted my sister to see the kitchen. I liked the kitchen so much because it reminded me of our home, where the kitchen was so big that my mother had fitted in two dining tables comfortably. One served mostly as a working area. She sewed on that table. We played Monopoly and cards on it. She often read her magazines at it. Our father liked to read his newspaper at the table on cold winter days. In summer, it was the veranda. But, best of all, we prepared to bake at this table because it was closest to the stove. The second table, placed more centrally, was mainly for meals. Meals, and sibling fights over allotted portions of food. I hated those shared meals because no matter how hard I tried I never mastered the art of chewing as fast as my elder brother. Well, my daughter would have no-one to fight with over rations of food. This kitchen was big enough for us to have two tables, just as in our original home.

After the visit with my sister, the occupant said, 'You will not regret this, I tell you. White people here just leave you alone. I don't even know them. Everyone minds their own business here.'

*

As we made our history driving in front of the movers' truck from Berea to Bellevue East on that last Sunday of March, I could not tell who was more excited, my daughter or me. She knelt on the back seat of the car producing an exhilarated running commentary, and having an imaginary conversation with the truck driver. Even our sea-green granny of a Toyota Corolla drove like a juvenile on that day.

After everything had been off-loaded I made us a snack and dashed to the office. By the time we returned home it was dark and I felt it would be rude to knock on a neighbour's door after dark just to greet them. I promised myself that I would rise early the next day so I could introduce myself to my neighbour and fell asleep. The thought that I was sharing a wall with a stranger permeated my dreams.

The morning did not work out as planned. It was just after 6 pm when we arrived home and I approached my neighbour's gate and buzzed before I unlocked the door to ours. I told her who I was before she reached the gate in order to unfurl the creases that inhabited her forehead as she walked from her front door to the gate.

She offered us a seat, called for 'Veronica' and promptly told us, 'My maid Veronica will make you tea.' When Veronica arrived in the lounge she went down on her knees in front of her madam. She greeted us, shook our hands and then departed to make us tea.

Elna started to interrogate me. By now I had been in Johannesburg for six years. I had become familiar with this interrogation dubbed 'getting to know you' by many white people I had met. I was frequently irritated by being interrogated at dinners, meetings, workshops and conferences. I discussed this with a white friend. She explained to me that in her culture it was a polite thing to do. When you meet someone, you show them you are interested in their lives by asking questions about their work. I wanted to know why this cultural practice was conducted as if they were talking to subjects in their research sample? And often after the declaration, 'Oh I won't even try to pronounce your name.' I told her that in my experience being asked about my work rather than who I was, was just irritating because my work was not my identity but rather the product of the limited choices apartheid made available to me. And, a white person who asked me questions was suspicious, was behaving like the police, or some official who assumed authority over me the minute they decided that my name was not worth an attempt at a proper pronunciation. I took an instant dislike to such individuals.

Those were the years when it was still acceptable to talk about the legacy of apartheid. But, back to Elna's lounge.

'Where do you work?' Elna asked.

'I work in an NGO, where do you work?' I asked, looking her straight in the eye.

'I work in an office.' Before Elna could say anything I said, 'What work do you do in the office?' I willed myself to maintain the unsmiling face which is very hard to hold onto when you are playing a game. I was so glad Nala had agreed to go to the kitchen with Veronica.

'I am a PA.'

I asked, 'You know, I have never understood the difference between a PA and a secretary. What it is?'

Elna stood up and went to rearrange her ornaments in the display cabinet. With her back to mine I could smile. Gotcha!

I had a few variations on my response to this getting-to-know-you interrogation. It depended on who was asking the questions, and of course my mood. For Elna I chose the discomfort-inducing version, since she was my neighbour. My best was the silencer version because of its efficacy. I used the unprintable, killer version only when my greatest desire was to strangle the person concerned.

When Veronica and Nala came back to the lounge,

a handsome boy who looked, at most, a year older than Nala was in tow. His teeth were as white as his eyes and lit his face when he smiled. He was Veronica's nephew and lived with her in the backroom. Mdu and Nala were already 'best friends'.

Between sips of tea Elna and I agreed that we would do as her brother had suggested. (Elna's brother was the one selling me the house.) Each month I would give Elna a cheque valued at R2 100 for occupational rent until the papers were finalised. She informed me that she would continue to park in our driveway until the house was transferred to me, after which she would find an alternative. Mdu walked home with us to play with Nala. I let them part after I had fed and bathed them. I went to the back of the house, shouted Veronica's name and handed Mdu to her over the wall that separated our semis.

It was not a week to meet the neighbours. I was terribly busy at work. I wondered if anyone had tried to come to our house to greet us. I wondered in fact whether this was common courtesy in these parts. I had established that the neighbour I shared a driveway with worked for Sun Couriers. The driveway being right next to my bedroom, I heard his car come in and leave. It woke me up at night and in the small hours of the morning. We never met, until months later when a neighbourly concern brought us face to face.

*

When we woke up on Sunday morning I had two things in mind: the 'SOLD' sign on the front patch of my garden under the jacaranda tree, and introducing myself to my neighbours. After breakfast I decided to start with the sign. With Nala in tow I walked into the garden and began removing the sign. As I was explaining to Nala why I was taking down the sign, I heard, in a reprimanding tone, 'Don't do that!'

Startled, I looked up. Elna was standing there, clearly looking at us.

'Good morning to you. Are you talking to me?'

'Yes, I said don't do that. That sign is not supposed to be taken down until three months after you've been in the house.'

'Thank you for the information.' I said and continued to uproot the sign. Of course I had to explain to my daughter why I was going against a neighbour's advice to which she responded, 'I think it's a stupid rule too, Mama.'

My neighbour stood there muttering something to herself, something I was happy I could not hear. The idea of meeting the other neighbours evaporated instantly.

Nala and Mdu continued to be 'bestest' friends, as Nala liked to say. Veronica and I had our chats during the just-before-bedtime-over-the-wall handover. The children decided at whose house they would be fed and bathed. We focused on safe landings on either side.

Veronica had worked for Elna and her brother since Elna's daughter was a toddler. The daughter was now in her late teens and her frequent verbal battles with her mother crossed the walls. They both were very comfortable screaming. Veronica said that sometimes they had fist fights. Veronica coughed constantly. I asked her about it and she told me that she had TB which she attributed to the leaking, uncarpeted back room without a ceiling that she said Elna was refusing to fix. My back room was structurally as uninhabitable as Veronica's. I told every single doorbell buzzer enquiring about a back room to rent that the backroom was not for rental. Other buzzers pleaded with such desperation that I let them view the room in the hope that they would be convinced of its uninhabitability. The opposite happened. Soon I knew that the correct answer for these buzzers was, 'I have a tenant already. Sorry.'

After the 'SOLD' sign saga, we moved on to the driveway drama and stayed there for the longest time. Elna used to park her car in front of my garage in such a manner that I could not drive out. If she arrived first in the afternoon she would park in a way that meant there was no room for me to get to the garage. At first when this happened I just let it be, telling myself that she was so used to having her brother there that she was operating as if he was still around. But when she parked me in I would knock on her door to tell her I needed to drive out. She would tell me not to disturb her. I would buzz and shout until she came out to move her car. Her behaviour really surprised me. One day I asked Veronica what kind of person Elna was. She had a simple answer, 'Oh, don't mind her. She has been unhappy since her husband died. Do you know a woman who has fist fights with her own daughter?'

'So why do you continue working for her?' I asked.

'I know her too well. She is so used to me that she knows that she would not get someone who would understand her as I do. So I stay with her.'

One Sunday when Elna had parked me in again, I

went to buzz her doorbell. Each time she did this I was shocked. Her response was that she was still in bed because it was a Sunday afternoon and I should leave her alone because I didn't even know how to speak English.

'*Sprechen Sie Deutsch?*' I asked.

'What did you say?'

'*Verzeihen Sie ngithi njengoba uzenza ngcono kangaka nje mfazi ndini ukhuluma izilimi ezingaki ke wena, siyazi wansondo, ukhala ungashayiwe nje?*'

The woman who was sleeping was right at the gate by the time I finished this sentence. She shouldered her way past me to the driveway, moved her car and told me not to speak to her ever again. I told her never to park me in ever again. Then, I stated the obvious: your brother is gone, I am now the owner of this space, I am merely doing you a favour by letting you use the driveway. She sounded very confident when she responded.

'The house is not yours until it's been legally transferred. Who knows if you can afford it?'

*

Sunset before 6 pm – the most depressing thing about winter – had successfully immersed itself into our daily lives on that June evening when a piercing scream shot through our lounge and I jumped off my beanbag in response. Without a thought, I flung Nala on my back and found keys to the front door and headed in the direction of the sound, the semi of the Sun Courier neighbour.

When I arrived at the source of the distress there

were already two neighbours there. I recognised faces from the few occasions I had driven out of our driveway at the same time as they had. A young black woman sitting on the pavement, tears streaming uncontrollably down her face, was telling a story of how a man had been trying to pull her to the side of the road to rape her, gun in hand. By the time she finished, she had a wad of tissues in her hand, an offer to be driven home, a volunteer who was going to call the police and four other neighbours on hand. So, in the dimness of an early winter evening I shook hands with six white neighbours I had not met in just over two months. One of them, with a large grin on her face, instructed me never to respond to an SOS scream with my baby on my back ever again. Another suggested a community meeting to discuss our safety. Another one informed me she was not going to try to pronounce my name. Another one said something to my baby.

*

July ended on a Wednesday that year. That was in my mind because I was to spend that Wednesday and Thursday working in the Northern Province and I was concerned about my monthly bills. Even before the car that dropped me off had disappeared from our road, Elna was in my house. (The front door was open as I was sorting my suitcase, Nala's bag and Nala. The poor child travelled with me on local trips.)

'You go away and not tell me and now you are in arrears. Where is the cheque?'

'*Angizwanga?*' I asked. I had heard her loud and

clear. I think I was so dumbfounded by her that the question came out spontaneously.

'I said, where is the cheque? You have not paid rent for the end of July. Have you forgotten you are just renting?' Her voice was getting louder with each sentence. Nala came and held tightly onto my pants.

I said, 'Go and tell your brother that I refuse to give you a cheque because you are rude.' I took my cheque book out of my handbag and waved it in her face.

'The neighbours are talking …' Then she hesitated, something un-Elna like. 'About your disappearances.'

That's the only time in my life I remember feeling fury escape through the pores of my skin. I struggled to breathe.

'They are also wondering if you can afford the house.'

I took one look at Elna and emitted a demonic shout from the bottom of the well of all my anger spirits. It was just one word: 'O … U … T!'

Nala cried for many minutes after Elna left our house. Fear and fury mingled. I did my best to explain to a four-year-old what had just happened.

On Saturday I met my Sun Courier neighbour. For the first time we were on the driveway at the same time. We greeted each other and he quickly proceeded to tell me that he would not be going to work that day, and as I would have noticed, he also worked on Saturdays, but because someone broke into his house and took his wallet and radio while he was fast asleep, he was waiting for the police to come. Had I heard anything? My head was spinning with all this information. Here was a neighbour whose snores I heard at night, whose face I had never set my eyes on, whom I was relieved to finally see, asking me if I had not heard the burglar who had robbed him in his sleep. I realised that it was not the time for me to introduce myself, or ask him his name. I empathised, wished him luck with the police and went my way. I was grateful for the unsightly double burglar bars on all our windows.

Elna's brother was at my door on Sunday, the fourth day in August. I offered him a seat and told myself to stay calm. This is how he began, 'I think you and Elna should really try to get on well together. You are neighbours ...' I stopped him right there, and continued to calm myself. I had one question for him: would he prefer that I mail his cheque or would he like to come and pick it up himself? He opted for the latter. 'Then call me and make an appointment each time.' He said he would and left. He did, until October when the transfer was finalised.

*

As I drove into the garage one evening, I noticed a lump of a body right next to the back entrance of our home. I was relieved that my daughter was fast asleep on the back seat. The man was painted in blood. It was hard to tell the source. He was breathing, moving and thankfully groaning appropriately. I asked him if he could walk and told him I would call an ambulance. He said he could walk and I should not call the ambulance – 'Please, my sister. Please.' To go against the wishes of a well-mannered man who is covered in blood seemed as inappropriate as singing off-key in a duet. Then, as if on cue from a director, he configured himself into a determined, groaning-less-and-less, brisk-walking machine. To my surprise, he remembered which way to turn.

I walked next to him to the end of the driveway, all the while expecting him to collapse. At the street he thanked me, took a left turn and, robot-like, walked away. I waited until his frame disappeared from sight before going back to the car to carry my beloved sleepy lump into the house. It's a weird feeling that: to have nearly found a corpse next to your garage.

*

The Nala and Mdu situation was working out perfectly. At the flat in Berea, the boy across the corridor had left many of Nala's toys broken. The two of them seemed unable to negotiate each other's auras with harmony. There was so much *snot en trane* when they were together. His parents and I soon agreed that the juice was not worth the squeeze. Mdu was a gentle boy who liked to wear Nala's dresses and skirts and played with dolls. They were inseparable. And they soon learned how to scale up and over the wall on their own.

During our Berea days, I had taught Nala to cry on the balcony as loudly as she needed to, whenever she needed to. I don't know what other parents do with tantrumic two-year-olds. That worked for me. When we arrived in the house in April one of Nala's first questions was where she was meant to go to cry. I said she must use the veranda at the back. This is the crying-screaming-and-shouting-and-talking-about-whatever-is-upsetting-me-right-now kind of crying that children of that age have perfected to an art. One Saturday morning as I was hanging clothes on the line at the back, Nala had such a session. Elna promptly came to her veranda, listened and watched for a while, then said to me, 'This is my proof. You are abusing this child. I am going to report you to the social workers.' Peg after peg, I hung my clothes and gave her silence.

Soon after that event my estate agent called me into the office. The bond had been processed. It was time, I thought, to execute my first unprovoked act towards Elna. It was an act I had been dreaming about each time Elna did her thing in the driveway. Elna was home before me on that day. It was one of those days when she had left enough space for me to park in my garage. When I buzzed her and told her it was me she said, 'What do you want?'

I said, very slowly, fully enjoying myself, 'I want you to come out of your house and move your car out of my driveway right now.'

I was unprepared for her response when she appeared at the gate and said, 'I am willing to pay you for parking until my brother has broken down our wall to make space for me to park on my yard.' I nearly fell over.

'No, I do not want your money. I want your car out of my driveway. Now!' I waited in joyful silence.

She parked on the street that night and the few nights that followed until the weekend when her brother came and started breaking the wall down. She dared not park on Sun Courier neighbour's side. I doubt she even asked him. I never once saw the two of them in conversation. After the demolition work had begun I let her back in again. It took her brother many more weekends before she could park right in front of her own house, behind a gate.

*

The exodus of whites from our part of Bellevue East was not as massive as I had heard it being reported in other areas. Elna moved out four years later. I baked for Veronica and Mdu's farewell. Our complexion has definitely gotten darker over the last ten years and there are more children in the streets. A man who recently moved in told me when I went to welcome him to the area that he was from KwaZulu-Natal, but I could tell that his accent was that of Ndebele speakers from beyond the Limpopo.

Those of us who have stayed on are staying put, in all our colours. We love our funny triangular suburb. Our homes with their fantastical pressed ceilings. I doubt we could afford to go anywhere else. Our jacaranda trees continue to inspire purple passages of prose and poetry. And we remain proudly un-boomed.

Elna, Veronica and Mdu are fictitious names to protect the identity of the real individuals.

Makhosazana Xaba, a former writing fellow at WISER, is the author of *these hands,* a volume of poetry. She is the winner of the 2005 Deon Hofmeyr Award for Creative Writing.

De Korte Street

Tom Odhiambo

My wife and I live on De Korte Street. To be exact, at
the corner of Station and De Korte streets, Braamfontein. We live in a two-room flat in one of the many
off-campus university residences. It is small, but comfortable and convenient for the two of us. Although the
noise of traffic on the street below is a nuisance during
the weekend, it doesn't worry us much during the week
because we both spend most of the time at work.

We came from Kenya to study, got married and have
settled here, for the time being. The choice to study for
a postgraduate degree in a foreign land was a difficult
one, for both of us. Equally difficult was the choice to
get married, thousands of miles away from our relatives.
But we do not regret either of these choices; our lives
may not be what we dreamed of as young people, but
probably they are better than they could have ever been
had we stayed back home.

After completing our PhDs at the University of the
Witwatersrand, we took up jobs in different fields. My
wife is a programme manager for a nongovernmental
organisation; I work as a researcher at the university. In
the evening, I am a warden in charge of three small

university halls of residence, which are separate from each other but administered as one. From hours spent in seminars or libraries or at my computer typing, I enter another world altogether back at the flat. A knock at the door means many things.

'Sir, I have locked myself out again.'

'My toilet is blocked. Please, can you call a plumber for me.'

Or a male student phoning to inform me that he has been receiving 'anonymous calls'. I spend most of my evenings calling out maintenance crews or counselling some of the students about the frustrations of university studies. Fridays can be a nightmare. I get knocks on the door late at night and in the wee hours of the morning. They are mostly to do with partygoers who have lost their keys or can't find their student cards and need to be let into the residence. My wife (or Mrs O) thinks that I am crazy to have accepted this extra job. But I like the fact that I live near my place of work. I do not have to suffer the misery of Johannesburg traffic jams and when I am hungry, I can hurry home to make myself a hot meal! Because she often has to take the bus or a taxi to work, she does not like my defence of this 'night watchman's' job! Yet we both seem to be happy about things as they are now.

*

I first met Mrs O some time in 1997, when she was still Ms M. I was a third-year student majoring in education at a university in the Rift Valley Province of Kenya. She was a first-year student also majoring in education. We were more acquaintances than friends for those two years in the Rift Valley. I left the university and went to teach in the countryside in western Kenya. I met her again when she arrived at Wits in 2001, a year after I had got here. I guess being in an alien land and having known each other before made it easier for us to become lovers. We got married here in Johannesburg after about five years of living together. But it wasn't an easy road to marital life. Although we are both Kenyans, she comes from one ethnic community, I come from another. Traditions, whatever that means, stood in the way. I am a child of two worlds. My mother's ethnic group is different from my father's. But since my parents separated when I was ten years old, I have grown up as a member of my mother's tribe. Mrs O's tribe does not very much trust people from my mother's tribe. Here was my dilemma. Then, when I met my future parents-in-law, I was alone – something that 'African traditions' do not take to kindly. But being in love makes you take immense risks. Eventually, though, it was the tact of the future Mrs O that smoothed the way in the negotiations with her parents on such matters as deferring payment of lobola to a future date; and I was accepted as a son-in-law, even when the consent for the marriage had to be given on the phone by a father-in-law from somewhere in the countryside of eastern Kenya.

*

I have police officers for neighbours: there is a police post next to the block of flats where I live. But they are not the most neighbourly of characters. I know what police work is like in Johannesburg from the stories of gunfights that make up the daily menu of evening news and newspaper headlines in the morning. I know I am meant to feel secure because of these neighbours, but given the character of Johannesburg, the police may mean danger rather than security. I live with the fear of a gunfight erupting next door to my block of flats at any time. My fears have been made worse by the cries for mercy from those who happen to find themselves booked into the police post as the officers extract information from them using not-so-legal methods. It makes a mockery of all the talk about a new dispensation, constitutional and human rights for all South Africans. Things can remain deceptively the same even in this so-called new dispensation.

*

I have lived in and around Braamfontein for almost the entire time I have been in South Africa. The formerly thriving business district has also acquired the distinction of having become another 'unsafe' area of Johannesburg – but has not reached the notoriety of its immediate neighbour Hillbrow. One is advised to be careful when walking in Braamfontein especially after work hours – in the evenings. In the year 2000 when I first arrived at Wits, I used to walk to the off-campus residence of Parktown Village One by myself as late as 9 pm in the evening. But things change. Nowadays, to walk from the main campus to Parktown is to test the patience of the gods of the street. Criminals are on the prowl, so goes the common warning. Yet I would say Braamfontein has been kind to me. I have never been a victim of crime since I arrived there. But I know people who have been relieved of their cellphones or wallets or made to withdraw money from an ATM at gunpoint. I guess life in this city on the move is about knowing what to do, where to do it and when to – these have been my tools of survival.

*

'*Star, Star!*' is a cry I have to endure from Monday to Friday. Though on Friday it changes to, '*Star, Guardian, Mail & Guardian!*' Language barriers have stifled many of the attempted conversations between this vendor of news and me, but we get along all right, or so I think, even when it is a struggle to make him understand that I would prefer a copy of the *Sunday Independent* on Sundays. How I wish I knew some Zulu! This man must have an interesting story to tell about his life on De Korte Street, I always think. What does he make of the newspapers and magazines published in English which he may wish to but cannot read, the daily traffic of vehicles and people, the motor vehicle accidents at the junction of De Korte and Station streets, the drag of the day as the hours slip by? Is it boring for him to sit in the same place every day from 6 am till 6 pm? But since we cannot chat, most of the time we simply look at each other and exchange the newspaper and the coins. In silence; a silence that haunts me every time I meet him. Whenever I see him, I think, 'You have lived in South Africa for over six years and can barely speak three words of Zulu or Sotho or Xhosa.' This is an opportunity missed, I tell myself. Why can't I learn even the most basic of Zulu or Sotho or Xhosa? I just can't understand it. I do not know this man's name; yet he knows my wife and whenever he does not see me during the day, he offers her: '*Star*, for him.' I am sure he does not know my name. I have wondered what goes on in his mind. His questioning silence. His ready-made smile. His politeness as he asks me in a mixture of Zulu and unintelligible English to spare a few minutes and look after his wares so that he can rush to buy some edibles from the petrol station shop down the road. His face betrays disappointment on the days when I do not buy the newspaper. 'Pay tomorrow,' he offers on such days. He manages to conceal his unease as he coaxes me to join the community of 'credit-takers.' In his silence he seems even to have developed an extra sensibility enabling him to know when I will and will not buy '*Star*'. Does he have a wife or relatives or friends? Is there somewhere he retires to in the evening? Or is he one of the many nameless street people that we take as 'normally' living on the streets? I would like to ask him these questions, but how do I start a conversation?

*

'Barbershop-cum-Salon' is what the sign on the shop's door advertises. So, I naturally walk in expecting a haircut. It is a risky venture sitting in this place for any period of time because this shop is exactly at the junction of De Korte and Station streets. That is one of the two major accident spots on De Korte Street, the other being the intersection between Jan Smuts Avenue and De Korte. The barbershop is a replica of several that have sprouted up along the length of De Korte and in

other parts of Braamfontein. These are small affairs in
size. But they are quite creative, in many senses. The
murals on the outer walls of these barbershops remind
me of such shops in the other major African cities I
have visited, Nairobi, Kampala and Dar es Salaam. The
proprietor of *my* shop has opted for a drawing of 'father
and son in conversation' – as if he is advising his son,
who will grow up in South Africa as a refugee, about the
hazards of being born and bred in foreign lands; and
what it takes to survive. On the door front hangs the
'Indomitable Lions' T-shirt, on sale. This gives away his
nationality – Cameroonian. But some of the members
of the extended 'family' are from other African countries. At least one of the barbers and a hairdresser are
from the Democratic Republic of Congo and Nigeria,
and the others Zimbabwe and Zambia.

I saunter into the shop for a haircut. '*Bonjour,*' a
young man of about 25 greets me. 'Good morning,' I
reply. 'What type do you like?' he asks in English, pointing to the generic black American haircut chart pasted
on the wall. I shake my head and start to describe how
I would like my hair to be cut. I do not get what I asked
for, but I get to know that he is a refugee from the DRC;
that he has a degree in electronic communication (I
guess he meant electronic engineering); that the rest of
his family is still in the DRC; that apart from working as
a barber, he also repairs computers; that he is in fact
also in charge of the Internet café, housed in the back
room of the shop; and that he is 'saved' by the blood of
Jesus. I am offered 'cheap' (his words) music down-
loaded from the Internet; I can buy the latest 'Nollywood' (Nigerian) movies (the trick is to ask for disk one

and two because most of the movies are recorded in parts on different disks) or an 'Arsenal Football Club' kit. 'It is original, brother,' he assures me as if he has read my mind wondering about 'fake' or '*fongkong*'. Of course I can only afford the cost of the haircut and promise to be back next time with a few extra rands to buy one of the many items on sale. As I leave, he hands me a photocopied leaflet advertising 'Tailoring and Loundry Services'. I presume the latter is meant to be 'Laundry'. 'So,' I ask him, 'what exactly is this shop?' Calmly he lets me know that I can get everything and anything from the shop. 'Just order.' I can sympathise with him, but also feel privileged that unlike him, I don't have to claim my refugee-ness in order to convince the Department of Home Affairs to allow me to stay in South Africa. I know that unlike him I can go back home to Kenya if and when I wish. But like him, I know the precariousness of life in Africa, which is why he is here. Somewhere in my heart, I silently pray that I never become a refugee like him.

*

A recent advert that has become popular in the print media sports the phrase 'born to shop' accompanied by a picture of a black youth. What a blessed generation! It is not surprising that shops all over Johannesburg compete to catch any prospective shopper's attention. In fact it is very difficult to avoid 'shopping' or buying something in Johannesburg because almost everything is offered at a discount or on credit – whether one needs it or not. Credit or buy-now-pay-later are as much available as the goods on offer themselves. When I was first employed, Mrs O could not understand why I had torn and thrown away the offer of a credit card from my bank. She said, 'You are not ambitious.' I retorted, 'I was born in poverty, and I very much fear to grow old into poverty.' For some time 'credit' became part of our supper talk. But that came to an end when she became employed and was offered a credit card. Mrs O wanted a car most. She wished we could live in the suburbs. She would have preferred us to go on holiday once a year. 'Could we please be eating out at least twice a week?' she posed. I wanted these things too. But I had been brought up in a household where you didn't spend someone else's money. Borrowing was a sin. I was tempted to agree with Mrs O. But as she settled into her job and the demands of relatives back at home increased, and we adopted a new lifestyle (we ate out at least once a week), she realised that she needed to save, and I was saved from explaining why I wasn't 'ambitious enough'. But that hasn't saved me from having to explain to a few newly arrived Kenyans why I have been in Johannesburg for 'more than three years and yet you don't have a car'. I have promised myself that should I settle back in Nairobi, I will buy a car. The damned car!

*

There is something alluring about the Mandela Bridge. Is it the sheer size of the bridge? Or is it the promise of something 'new' to be experienced in Newtown? Or could it be that it appears a little bit out of place; odd? However, there are few landmarks around this part of

Johannesburg to rival the Mandela Bridge. The charms
of the Market Theatre and the Newtown cultural pre-
cinct await whoever crosses the bridge into town. Who
wouldn't be charmed by the grand old man Madiba! I
have crossed it by car and on foot on several occasions,
and each time I marvel at the dreams that it stands for. It
indeed connects two worlds; the drab community of business and academy in Braamfontein and the creativity and
culinary world of Moyo, the Market Theatre and the
South African Breweries World of Beer, among many
other places of entertainment and culture. In Newtown,
one senses, among the artists, actors, theatregoers, even
vagabonds, some kind of excitement about the energies
of cross-racial cultural renewal and cohabitation that the
new South Africa possesses. For me, the excitement of
what 'this place' *could* become – the dream of a humanity
without xenophobia, a world of conviviality – starts with
the Mandela Bridge. Vandals may have recently ripped
off parts of the bridge, but it, like the old man himself,
endures. It remains a bold statement of aspiration and
hope in a country that has been part of me for the past
six years. One of my precious memories in Jozi will be
the overwhelming sensation of being among the first
people to use the bridge, a sense of coming into contact
with Mandela every time I walk from my noisy street life
to the evening tranquillity of Newtown.

*

'*Hujambo bwana*,' [How are you, sir] I salute the short
darkish fellow in the five-metres-square tuckshop. My
hunch that he speaks Swahili is proved correct when he

responds, '*Sijambo.*' [Fine] The tuckshop is tucked in between other similar 'shops' – stalls in reality – that have sprouted on Biccard and adjacent streets. From De Korte Street, I turn to my right into Biccard and enter a new world. This is the world of the so-called *amakwerekwere.* The foreigners. The aliens. The visitors. A world I have come to love because it is the world of those like me. They come in shades. Visitors on temporary permits who have simply taken leave to extend their stay. Refugees 'allegedly' running away from political persecution in their home countries. Students. Traders. Travellers en route somewhere. Men and women with horror stories of deprivation and death 'back at home'. Real stories and made-up ones. Those found on Biccard Street, however, are mainly from Nigeria, Cameroon, Tanzania, or the Democratic Republic of Congo. There are also Ugandans, and a few Mozambicans. My fellow Kenyans are in short supply here. But it is to the Tanzanians that I head. I know two of them who used to sell cigarettes and candies outside the university gates. We had become familiar with each other and because we shared a language, Swahili, I felt then and still feel as if we share a fate – we are all foreigners here, aren't we? These guys are quite friendly and charming. Maybe it is this mien of theirs, embellished with a permanent smile and camaraderie, that enables them to become small-time successful businessmen – they are generally all men; if there are women from their home countries, they are tucked into the background or hidden away in the hair salons. These migrants have turned this part of Braamfontein into a mini-Africa within South Africa. You can get *yam foofoo* or *gari* (dishes made from yams) and plantains from Nigeria in the groceries that also double as eateries; you can order the latest Senegalese attire (beloved of Africans obsessed with demonstrating their Africanness in their manner of dress); a pint of 'home' beer can be purchased, if you know how to ask for it; and the latest Hollywood release is available on DVD before you can watch the movie in comfort in a cinema in Rosebank. The refrain will be: 'It's ligal my broda,' without the slightest hint of irony! Not even the Nollywood copies I buy here all the time are authentic.

I wonder, of course, how the foods, the clothes, the DVDs from East, West and Central Africa cross the borders. With *makossa* and *kwasa kwasa* or *ndombolo* (popular West African and Congolese dance styles, respectively) beats in the background, you can haggle for everything from groceries to cosmetics to the 'cheapest calling rates to the rest of the world in town' to computer accessories in this 'little Africa'; it does not matter what the customer desires. It can be 'arranged'. What one needs can be fetched from a bar, a brothel or a hostel down the street, within minutes. There are middlemen and businessmen and hawkers, of all races and colours and nationalities, doing business here all day long, all night long. Some are innocuous, sitting quietly in the expensive BMWs, Benzes and Volkswagens parked along the dirty street; whilst others holler to the potential customers about 'deals'. Men (and the hidden women) seeking their fortunes in ways legal and not so legal – providing ready-made headlines with which lazy Johannesburg journalists mock and lambast the Department of Home Affairs and the government for 'letting in all these foreigners to ruin our country'. The moment some of these men and women from north of the Limpopo manage to acquire their fortunes, they will buy themselves into South Africanness – the phrase 'permanent residence', like the fate of most of these men and women, floats loudly on the wind down the street. It is the magic key to supposed peace and prosperity for most of these fellow travellers. I see myself in this whirlwind of humanity and fortune-seekers. Am I not a fortune-seeker too, in search of the stronger rand? What draws me to this micro-Africa every weekend, I wonder? Is it really the groceries that I go buying there; is it the pirated copies of the latest Nollywood films (I have an academic interest in them too); or is it, like a lost member of a herd, the nostalgia of 'home', the sense of belonging to a group, a search for familiarity? Maybe.

*

De Korte Street has been my 'home away from home' for almost three years now. It is hemmed in by a big block of offices 'Just Letting' and a car parking lot also 'Just Letting' on the western end; and Argyle Centre, a student residence, and the National Health Laboratory Service on the eastern end. It takes about fifteen minutes to walk from the one end to the other. Along the way from the eastern end I pass by a Young Women's Christian Association hostel appearing neat and secure, just like the five-star Parktonian Hotel, sitting there as if challenging the cheap neighbouring former-offices-converted-into-flats to a duel. Signs announcing denominations and churches from windows atop the grocery stores and flats compete with all manner of washing hanging from lines and windows – eyesores mocking architects and town planners. As a one-way street, from the east to the west, it empties the Johannesburg central business district of thousands of people back to the suburbs and the townships. Whenever I crane my neck from the balcony of my flat to the farthest eastern end of the street that my eyes can reach, I can see, in one sweep, the changes that it has experienced recently. Buildings which previously had the 'For Sale' or 'Office Space' signs on them have been or are being renovated. Furniture stores, tuckshops, fast food outlets, nightclubs, student accommodation, flats, offices, colleges offering certificates and diplomas in all manner of studies are among the new occupants of previously vacant and abandoned buildings.

*

It is all a game of lotto, 'Tata ma chance.' You may win, you may lose, but keep trying. You may get lucky one day! There is lotto everywhere here in South Africa. All these schools promising young South Africans a bright future via education, the certificate- and diploma-peddling colleges, the university where I work with its bleak ancient-looking buildings a hundred metres away, the residences hosting those in search of an education and a dream in Jozi, the daytime eateries and tuckshops that also double as pool-table venues where young schoolboys and girls idle away the day trying their hands at illicit gambling, the sleepy and 'silent' newspaper vendor, the noisy students with their ghetto blasters and fancy disc-jockey machines in the hostels neighbouring mine, the not-so-friendly police officers whiling away another day, the car dealerships offering one and all a chance to drive into the new and future South Africa, the nightclubs that pour out Afro-beats all the night from Friday to Sunday, the gay clubs whose dancehalls reverberate with heavy-metal sounds all night long all weekend. All these places, peoples of different colours, tongues and origins, sounds of gunfire late in the night, smells of crashing car tyres, noises of merrymakers, have come to define De Korte Street. Mrs O and I have participated in this lotto. My feeling is that we haven't lost; but we haven't won millions either. The promise is still there, but we are going to pursue it elsewhere. Wits University, De Korte Street, Braamfontein, Johannesburg, South Africa, have all changed our lives. As I sit in my flat contemplating 'what next' after I leave South Africa in a few months' time, I wonder whether I would ever have had post-graduate schooling if I had remained in Kenya; would I have married Mrs O if fate hadn't thrown us together again here in a foreign land; exactly what would I have been if I hadn't come to South Africa in 2000? I have no answers to these questions. I am struggling with more questions about what to do when I leave for Kenya; how to account to friends and family for the years of absence; how to start afresh. Well, I console myself, if you have lived in Johannesburg you can live anywhere.

Tom Odhiambo is a former researcher at WISER. He is author of numerous articles on African popular literature.

Rock and Roll Marxists?

Jon Hyslop

I am a historian by trade. Not, one would have thought, a particularly risky business. After all, one might ask, what could be less dangerous than writing about (mainly) dead people? Although, that said, India's leading archaeologist has received death threats for suggesting that medieval Muslims did not demolish temples on the scale that Hindu fundamentalists claimed.

But the risk I want to take is of a different sort. It is to use my own experience to look at a particular moment in history, to make myself and people like me the subject of the investigation. In doing this I take three kinds of intellectual risk. Firstly, I look critically at my past self and the ideas that I once held – always a painful thing to do. Secondly, I set myself up for the scrutiny of others. South Africans love nothing better than to issue censorious character sketches of one another, and this provides a rare opportunity for anyone who would like to develop one of me. Thirdly, I take the risk which historians always do, which is to subject one's hard-won ideas to public scrutiny.

Historians like to start their inquiries with a question. This is mine. During the 1970s, a rather large number of young white English-speaking South Africans became politically radicalised against the apartheid system, and became attracted to ideas which can loosely be described as Marxist. Why did this happen? And where did it lead?

I was one of that generation and part of that process. Whether or not one sees it as an important phenomenon, it is something that should provoke a certain amount of curiosity. After all, white South Africans in the 1960s and 1970s were one of the most materially privileged populations on earth. Why should some of them have stopped believing in the social order that placed them in this position?

This essay is intended as a kind of historical inquiry. It is in no sense an apologia for myself or a demand for sympathy or admiration from the reader. Many autobiographical writings by South Africans have appeared in recent years which take as their themes, with varying levels of justifiability, the author's:

- heroism;
- moral integrity;
- indispensable role in the liberation struggle; and/or
- theoretical genius.

None of the above applies in my case. Physically, I am distinctly on the cowardly side. I have no interest in claiming to be more moral than anyone else; were that my concern in life I would have joined the clergy. I realised after a brief apprenticeship that I am not good at political activism. And I am not one of those who aspire to cabbalistic insight into the nature of the world. All I want to claim for myself is the professional competence and, hopefully, honesty, of the journey-man historian.

Let's turn then to our question. A good starting point is the cultural shock which Anglophone whites experienced at the moment of the Afrikaner nationalists' triumph in 1948. At the beginning of that year, white Anglophones were at a peak of their historical trajectory. For all of their history, their primary political identity had resided in their sense of being part of Britain's empire. While a new feeling of South Africanism had emerged with some strength since the 1920s, it lived within a context of loyalty to King and Commonwealth. For many of the 'English' their self-image was simply as the local franchise of the British Empire. They had enthusiastically supported Britain in the Second World War, and their military efforts had been appreciated in the metropolis. They were firmly allied with a faction of Afrikaners under Jan Smuts which had accepted reconciliation with imperial Britain. Smuts himself was an immensely influential world statesman who embodied the Union's international respectability.

With the advent of apartheid this self-image fell apart. The newly independent nations of Africa and Asia slowly but effectively brought about the isolation of Pretoria in the Commonwealth and Empire. And with the departure of South Africa from the Commonwealth in 1960-61, institutional links with Britain were shattered. This created a real identity crisis for young white Anglophones growing up in the 1960s. Although they were fascinated with Britain as a metropolis, it was no longer a plausible source of political identity. The sentimental attachment to the old country of an older generation began to look silly. Years after the advent of the South African republic, when Elizabeth II appeared on the television screen, my father would say, 'She's still my queen.' But I certainly didn't feel she was *mine*.

Yet the new Afrikaner state of Verwoerd and Vorster was even less attractive. The first two decades of the National Party's rule were characterised, amongst other things, by policies which aimed to replace Anglophones with Afrikaners in the state services and institutions. This version of affirmative action was immensely resented by the 'English'. I grew up hearing my family regale each other with tales of how friends and relatives had been forced out of positions in the civil service and the army, denied state contracts or pushed off institutional boards. Interestingly, I recall these conversations as being remarkably similar in form to current white conversations about 'empowerment' policies in the post-apartheid era.

Now all of this hardly constituted great social suffering, for the white Anglophones enjoyed vast material prosperity, which by the time of the 1960s economic boom made them one of the most affluent groups of people in the world. Nevertheless, it did mean that in an important way people like me grew up with the sense that the state was not our state. We felt we could never aspire to a career within its institutions.

Resentment of Afrikaner nationalist domination focused on the compulsory teaching of Afrikaans in English-medium schools, something which the more vigorous government ideologues hoped would lead to the cultural incorporation of Anglophones. Afrikaans teachers were pursued by *sotto voce* schoolboy ethnicist jibes.

What made this conflict complex though was that although the Anglophones were politically weak in relation to Afrikaners, they were also economically powerful. While the government was successfully managing a social revolution which would convert much of the Afrikaner lower middle class and working class into professionals, managers and entrepreneurs, this process was by no means complete. By and large, Afrikaners were still visibly poorer than Anglophones. The Anglophones' view of Afrikaners was inflected with a nasty class disdain – mocking their clothes, their manners, their accents.

Greatest of the resentments of the young Anglophones though was the imposition of compulsory military service for white males from the late 1960s. I recall my feeling of sheer dread when the military registration forms were dished out at school. Sometime later a team from the army arrived to conduct medical inspections; for some reason I was not summoned by the doctors. Friends reported that the main feature of the exam appeared to be a check on whether your testicles moved when you coughed. We certainly understood conscription as an imposition by Afrikaner authorities. Commanded by mainly Afrikaner officers and enforced by bullying noncommissioned officers, the South African Defence Force was loathed by many of those who had to serve in it. Hair-raising stories of physical punishment filtered back to our school locker room.

Many of those who went to the army were traumatised by their experience. A friend's brother died in the army of an illness he had tried to report to the officers. My contemporaries spun out their university studies to gain draft deferments. Many left the country to avoid the draft; a few became conscientious objectors. I was determined not to serve. During the 1970s, when the army was keen to have the dubious advantages of my soldierly services, I stayed out of the country. I was extraordinarily lucky – by the time I came back in the mid-1980s, I seemed to have slipped through the military's administrative system. But I still have nightmares in which the military police are looking for me.

There was, though, no necessary reason why this ethnically propelled social disaffection, on its own, should have turned young white Anglophones to radical political or intellectual stances in relation to the structure of South African society as a whole. For we were the children of a generation who – with distinguished exceptions – took the inequality between whites and Africans for granted. I remember upper-middle-class Anglophone society as being infused with racial ideology. As a child I recall listening to adults seriously discussing whether black people had differently shaped skulls from whites, and if so whether this meant they had smaller brains. I remember a family friend who worked on the mines explaining to me that Africans could only see pictures in two dimensions. This was standard conversational fare in suburban Johannesburg.

One of the great 'successes' of apartheid was in physically separating the worlds of white and black people, and thereby in undermining the possibilities of young whites experiencing any cross-racial empathy. My school was, like all others in the country, almost totally segregated; a handful of Chinese boys were the only exceptions in our all-white school world. The world of the suburbs was pristine, every road sign painted and verge trimmed. And, as most suburbanites preferred not to notice, every black person without a pass scooped up by a quietly patrolling police van. It was not until the early 1970s that significant numbers of black people began to get clerical jobs in the private sector, and not until the end of that decade that significant numbers began to reach the lower levels of management. University segregation was near-complete until it began to break down at the end of the 1970s.

The shift towards an understanding of the wider political context came, I think, from two sources, both of which are liable to be at a discount in South Africa today. The one was liberalism; the other the youth revolt and its 'Counterculture'.

Retrospective accounts of apartheid tend to ignore that liberals did manage to maintain elements of independent civil society institutions during the high apartheid years. If the more committed apartheid ideologues had totalitarian aspirations, they were never able to impose them in an unrestricted way. Liberals did sustain dissenting newspapers, anti-apartheid legal practices, a degree of academic freedom in some universities, and independent publishing, writing and theatre. Though these achievements may seem little set beside the vast brutalities of apartheid, they were I think

crucial to the subsequent political processes in South
Africa. A space for critical discussion and expression
which a fully totalitarian order would have prevented,
did survive.

I grew up reading, every weekday morning, the journalism of the *Rand Daily Mail*, in which writers like Benjamin
Pogrund and editors like Lawrence Gandar and Raymond
Louw, who faced state intimidation and prosecution,
determinedly denounced every aspect of apartheid policy
from conditions in prisons to forced removals. The very
first contact and political discussion I had with black
people of my own age was at a conference for school children organised by the stoutly liberal Institute of Race
Relations, at which the discussion centred on the Arusha
Declaration on the liberation of southern Africa made by
the Organisation of African Unity. A friend who was a
student leader recently recalled a moment during a student protest at Wits in the 1970s when the then vice
chancellor of the university, Guerino Bozzoli, climbed on
top of a fire hydrant and stated bluntly that people were
being killed in detention. The scientific critique of racial
ideology waged by Phillip Tobias severely discomfited
white received wisdom. I remember reading a Tobias
pamphlet as my crucial moment in questioning racial
ideology, and I know others had the same experience. All
sorts of criticisms can be and are made of South African
liberalism, but my memory of the era does not accord with
the current received wisdom that liberals solely engaged
in effete complicity with government. Be that as it may,
what was certainly the case was that liberal journalists,
teachers and activists were an important source of information for young people about the realities of apartheid.

But what I think really fired the emerging new white leftism was an interaction between this dawning political awareness and the personal upheavals sparked by the international Counterculture of the 1960s and 1970s. For young people in a claustrophobically controlled society, the slightest sense of discontent made the idea of 'sex, drugs and rock and roll' irresistibly appealing.

Even in the metropolitan countries, the conflicts of this era were pretty painful. An older generation reared in the hard school of the Great Depression and the Second World War, and committed to the values of hard work and self-discipline, clashed with the libidinal energies of a younger generation. Yet that was in the context of relatively liberal societies. In deeply reactionary and authoritarian South Africa, the lid was held on the pot that much tighter, and the build-up of pressure even greater as a consequence. The government was endeavouring to exercise comprehensive control over the socialisation of young white people. Every manifestation of contemporary youth culture was seen as a stalking horse for Communism (despite official Communism's own deep distaste for rock and roll music). Energetic state campaigns of legal repression against drug-taking were mounted. Radio programmes and talks by instructors at school camps and in the army warned of the dangerously subversive effects and (literally) diabolic messages hidden in the lyrics of The Doors.

These attempts at ideological steering were guaranteed to fail, and indeed to be counterproductive. I remember when, in the mid-1960s, the SABC banned the music of the Beatles after John Lennon had mooted the proposition that the group were more popular than Jesus Christ. For early teenagers like me this simply intensified the glamour of the group. As we listened to Beatle music on LM Radio, which broadcast from Portuguese-controlled Mozambique, we felt a (retrospectively absurd) subversive *frisson*. And the more overtly political end of rock music was a carrier of exactly the messages that the authorities wanted to repress. In fact anything the state was suspicious of seemed automatically interesting. After I heard, on an SABC programme, about what a bad influence a man called Bob Dylan was, I went out and bought some of his records. And, partly through Dylan's lyrics, I became increasingly interested in the US civil rights movement, and started thinking about the suggested parallels with the South African situation.

The white Anglophone youth was, sociologically, a prime candidate for the Counterculture. As elsewhere in the world, youth culture fed off two post-Second World War developments; the extended adolescence produced by greater access to high school and university, and the availability of disposable income to young people, which could be spent on clothes, music – and drugs. In South Africa, the extreme privilege of whites made these features even stronger. The length of time which some students took to get through their degree courses was notorious, while the levels of youthful affluence matched and exceeded those of metropolitan countries. White South African parents ended up paying for their children to engage in extended experiments in identity. And in many cases this produced results which were not what they wished for their offspring. While older-generation

Anglophones did not, by and large, go along with Afri-kaner nationalism's ideological engineering, they had conservative patterns of their own. Their own shaping in the colonial way of life of the 1930s and 1940s attached them to the values of that time and place. They wanted upstanding, Brylcreemed, blazer-wearing, conformist sons, and demure daughters who were wives-and-mothers in training. Suddenly and alarmingly, this was not what they were getting. The new music, the long hair and bright clothing of the young men and the incipient self-assertion of the young women, the pungent smoke wafting from the bottom of the garden, violently antago-nised them. To me and my friends, the Rolling Stones were the embodiment of the dissidence to which we aspired. My strongest image of my schooldays is probably of a Johannesburg garage in which my friend Alistair's band plays a truly appalling but wildly exciting rendition of 'Jumping Jack Flash'.

In a way, the state was quite shrewd in knowing that it could not control the modernist political energy of rock and roll. When, in a moment of dereliction, the censors allowed a screening of the movie of the massive hippy-era Woodstock concert, the Hillbrow cinema where it was showing was packed with kids who jumped up and down in the aisles when Jimi Hendrix played. A black rebel was suddenly the hero of the golden chil-dren of apartheid. And the anti-Vietnam War rhetoric of the movie had its impact. Faced with conscription, it dimly dawned on my friends and me that when Country Joe and the Fish sang, 'Be the first one on your block to have your boy come home in a box,' that boy might be one of us.

Schools too were places of generational conflict. Even those few schools that had a quotient of politically liberal teachers subscribed to extremely conservative ideas of self-presentation and behaviour and enforced them in an authoritarian manner. Trivial but, to teenagers, all-absorbing, micro-conflicts were waged. My school friends and I fought a steady campaign to grow our hair long against teachers and prefects determined to have it cut. I felt every centimetre that my hair crept down my neck as a triumph. Anti-authoritarian sentiments were nurtured by such petty conflicts. People who like the 'big picture' in historical explanation would dismiss such 'trivial' experiences. But what happens to individuals and to societies is ultimately inseparable. Political decision-making involves a sliding between personal experience and formal ideas which is seldom allowed for by the reason of political ideologues.

The youth culture not only widened the distance between young white Anglophones and the state but also involved conflicts which made them look more critically at the ideas of parents and teachers. This laid a generation open to a deeper revolution in their ideas. In the context of the universities of the 1970s the factors of anti-state sentiment and Counterculture came together with political upheaval to produce a new direction.

The development of the Black Consciousness Movement at the beginning of the 1970s, which not only asserted black political autonomy but also attacked white liberalism for its limitations, was traumatic but bracing. This did tend to produce some slightly ludicrous moments – it was almost as if the young white radicals wanted to be berated by black activists for their political inadequacies. I remember a meeting at which James Matthews, a Black Consciousness poet with a slightly intimidating personal presence, opened the proceedings by glowering fiercely at the assembled eager white students. James snarled, 'What a lot of blank faces …' and was met with adoring looks. But such confrontations were salutary. I do think that young whites who were exposed to the Black Consciousness Movement in that era were forced to think about race in a more complex way than any earlier (or indeed later) white dissenters.

Another factor which was important was the involvement of small, but very significant, groups of young whites in the new black trade unions of the 1970s. These erupted onto the scene with the Durban strikes of 1973. As soon as young whites began to make the effort to look around them, they saw the extraordinarily extreme poverty of that era. The idea that workers could do something to challenge this, and that middle-class people with skills could help, was vastly attractive.

Once again the repressiveness of the regime had its counterproductive effects. In the late 1960s and early 1970s, with the state seemingly ahead of all challenges, police could devote enormous attention to relatively minor forms of dissent. Student demonstrations were met with force. Writers of political articles in student newspapers were prosecuted. Although this created a climate of fear, it also tended to make people draw the most radical political conclusions about the nature of political power. I remember a student demonstration being confronted by scores of heavily armed policemen backed up by a mob of rightist students from Rand Afrikaans University. Such moments were 'truth events': growing up in the safe, clean suburbs, we had no idea of the monstrous power on which the social order was based. Now we saw it for ourselves. Shockingly, we realised that what was often no more than social experimentation could have dire consequences. And it did. Student leaders were deprived of passports, arrested, banned.

It was in this context that Marxism developed its appeal as an ideology. Part of this was a kind of oedipal rejection of older-generation liberals – to whom they in reality owed so much – by young radicals. Liberals were seen as patronising towards black political movements, as avoiding issues of class inequality and as insufficiently militant against a repressive state. The new generation felt that their mentors had betrayed them. Marxism appeared to provide the answers; capitalism was the root of all social problems; the state was its enforcer; the workers, now erupting onto the streets of South Africa, were the social force that would bring about socialist revolution.

And what a time for Marxism it was. The radicalisation of this generation was taking place at a moment in which, internationally, Marxist ideas were undergoing a renaissance. In the early twentieth century Marxism had been immensely intellectually productive, and remained so into the first decade of the Russian revolution. But as it became an official state ideology in the Soviet Union during the late 1920s, it increasingly lost this dynamism. Official Communism through the mid-twentieth century, all over the world, repressed intellectual creativity. By the 1960s, however, the discrediting of state Marxism as a result of the revelations of Stalin's purges and the Soviet invasions of Hungary and Czechoslovakia had opened a space for new kinds of Marxist analysis. French and German philosophers, British historians, 'Black Marxists', Latin American revolutionaries and (across the world) feminists all produced Marxist works of genuine intellectual innovation. By the early 1970s, such publications of the New Left were pouring off the international presses. Despite the best efforts of the censors, they were finding their way to South Africa.

Of course South Africa did have indigenous forms of Marxism, notably the tradition of the Communists in the African National Congress and the Unity Movement in Cape Town. Older activists from these movements were around. But I do think it is true to say that the new interest in Marxism did not come particularly strongly from them. The ANC and the South African Communist Party were still trying to re-emerge from the defeat of the 1960s. Moreover, South African official Communism maintained an unlimited credulity towards Soviet Marxism, which tended to make its supporters hostile to new ideas. The Unity Movement had a more intellectually vigorous tradition, but its somewhat paranoid political manner tended to isolate it. I do think therefore that much of the political thinking of the early 1960s (not only amongst whites but also within the ambit of the Black Consciousness Movement) can be understood as part of an international New Left.

It is hard to convey now the kind of intellectual excitement which young leftists of that era experienced. As one pored over Marxist texts there was a feeling of an understanding of the world falling into place. The discontent that you felt with all that you had been brought up to believe in was explained. Out of suburban ignorance, vistas of philosophy and history opened up. The experience was one of revelation.

This was not just a feature of life in South Africa. Internationally, the early 1960s and early 1970s were one of those rare moments in history when it seems that the world is going to shift on its axis. With economic crisis in the major capitalist economies, the defeat suffered by the United States in Vietnam, massive militant labour movements across the world, and the rise of new political insurgencies such as feminism and environmentalism, the left internationally could feel fervent.

Such moments have their benefits, for they open up the imagination to roam out of existing constraints. But they also have their dangers – political millenarianism is akin to religious millenarianism. Change is conceived as absolute and miraculous, and its result as perfection. The battle is of absolute evil versus absolute good. The millenarian position generates boundless energy, but not always analytical clarity and never any sense of political practicality. Both in South Africa and in the wider world, radicals experienced the world in a way which was as much based on blind faith as it was on their purportedly materialist analyses.

In the mid-1980s, after studying and working for ten years in the UK and elsewhere, I was back in my home town. It was my place in the world, where I wanted to be. I had found a real calling. I was working towards completion of a PhD and teaching undergraduates at Wits University. And I loved doing it. I had at last, after much confusion and waste of opportunity, come to realise that an academic career was what I really wanted, and committed myself to the vast amount of work that it required. But circumstances were dramatic. A revolution was raging in South Africa. There were constant battles between students and police on campus, militant mass meetings, and detentions of staff and students. Whiffs of tear gas hung over the university.

While I had been away, many of my generation had achieved remarkable things, on the basis of the ideas they had formed in the previous decade. Some had played crucial parts in the formation and organisation of trade unions. A few were prominent in oppositional movements. A number had become civil rights lawyers. Others worked as dissident publishers or journalists or in radical educational NGOs. Oppositional theatre had developed to a point where it was a phenomenon attracting world attention.

At the universities, at least in the social sciences, a big shift had taken place. The radical students of the previous years were now the junior and middle-rank academic staff. Marxist ideas had become central to many of the courses. Teaching was exciting work. The many black working-class students who by now had broken through the barriers to enrol at the university, were highly politicised and avid to talk about ideas with their teachers. The brightest of the young white students were engaged and sharp. It was a joy to teach in such circumstances. Academic conferences were riven with political debate. A stream of new historical research and writing was flowing, giving rise to the popularisation of a new history of the country. Deluded or not, I felt I was 'making a difference'.

There was, though, an interesting difference between the white student radicals of the 1980s and those of the previous generation. By the 1980s, the ANC and SACP had successfully brought about their hegemony in the oppositional movement through their international profile, underground operations and guerilla activities. The United Democratic Front and its affiliated organisations became a crucial organisational vehicle for opposition. This did create the political momentum which was indispensable to change. But it also tended to produce a political culture which was considerably more dogmatic. A friend used to refer to one particular leader of the white left as *'Die Beampte'*, an Afrikaans term for civil servant, thus nicely capturing the authoritarian style involved. I don't dispute that a more structured form of political movement was necessary and inevitable. But I did feel that it produced a shift towards a lesser degree of intellectual and cultural creativity.

In a sense, though, South Africa in the mid-1980s was kept in a self-contained ideological bubble by its combination of revolutionary upheaval and enforced international isolation through sanctions. The warfare between security forces and insurgents in the streets, the heavy hand and the stupid propaganda of a state committed to defending the status quo at all costs, and the emergence of the world's fastest-growing and most radical labour movement made Marxist interpretations of the world appear more than plausible. And despite the fact that even the Communist movement in most of the world was by then well aware of the fraying of the Soviet Union and its satellites, local Communists and ANC supporters retained an unshaken faith in the USSR as a social model that had largely disappeared in the USSR itself. Even those 'dissident' Marxists amongst whom I'd include myself, who detested the repressiveness of the Soviet regime, tended to believe that it was somehow possible to transform it into something better.

For all my sympathy with the revolutionary upheaval going on around me, something scary began to happen to me. I was put to teaching sociological theory and asked to teach not just Marx, but other schools of social thought as well. As I began to relate the ideas I was discussing with the students to what was happening around me, I slowly realised that I was no longer sure that Marxism explained the world quite as well as I had believed. I was watching a revolution. But I found that this, exactly the sort of event that Marxism should be best equipped to explain, didn't quite fit the theories. The behaviour of political move-ments and trade unions seemed increasingly to me to be driven by factors other than those which Marxist analyses – whether their own or those given by academic sympathisers – suggested. These analyses simply didn't cut it in accounting for the subjective decisions of politi-cal leaders. And the apartheid state, which we relent-lessly analysed, did not seem to do the things that a sensible agent of the bourgeoisie would do. The inde-pendent interests of generals, bureaucrats and politicians seemed to be much more important in how power was exercised than I'd allowed for.

Of course, at the same time, Marxist scholars all over the world were creating ever more complex models of explanation in their attempts to cope with their own realities. The difficulty was that, given the inability of Marxists to agree with each other, many of their disputes amongst themselves turned out to overlap with disputes amongst 'bourgeois' theorists. Crude Marxism had a clear identity, but at the price of skating over conceptual ambiguities and historical evidence. Once Marxism became sufficiently empirically or theoretically subtle, it tended to lose what advertisers would call its 'unique selling point'. I began to feel that that which was valid in Marxist sociology and history was not necessarily Marxist, and that that which was Marxist in it was not necessarily valid. My research too, deepened this feeling. I successfully wrote a PhD in a broadly Marxist framework, but I found that my evidence fitted poorly with the Marxist state theory which had been my starting point.

In the wider world things were taking a very different turn. The tough prescriptions of free-market physicians had turned the 'crisis' of capitalism around. Internationally, the millenarianism of the left had faded and its proponents turned either to careerism or to wailing in the wilderness. Trade union numbers fell and left political parties moved towards the political centre. The left had, not for the first time in its history, failed to allow for the recuperative powers of capitalism. The working classes of the Soviet bloc countries turned out to be eager to overthrow the dire police states which constituted 'really existing socialism'. The Marxist intellectual wave was ebbing internationally.

I gradually moved to a view that while Marxism provided some important sociological ideas, it attached to these a kind of political theology that did not follow from them. Marxism could generate powerful historical analyses, but its political prescriptions tended to be driven by wish-fulfilment. I became convinced by Max Weber's view that political decisions are based on values and that those values are ultimately not subject to logical arbitration.

The attraction of Marxism, I came to think, lay in a just horror at poverty and inequality. But Marxists refused to recognise that this was an ethical, subjective, value-based choice. They wanted Marxism to be a total philosophy and science that explained everything. And this it could not be. I retained the belief that material inequalities are at the centre of the questions that society has to deal with. But I no longer believed that Marxism has the political or the economic solutions.

With the end of apartheid, South Africa entered a world that was very different from the one that had initially isolated it. Marxist intellectuals often became woefully incoherent. Assurances of doctrinal purity often went along with pragmatic policy proposals, many of which were complete non sequiturs. Many of those who continued to go to the Marxist church no longer believed. It became a sentimental rather than an intellectual investment. Some made the discovery of the dominant academic trend of the 1990s, poststructuralism. But this tended to become a new kind of faith, in a manner strangely at odds with its proponents' claim to be non-prescriptive. A handful of others clung on to the Marxist faith in forms that were redolent of crank religious sects.

Now, more than a decade after 1994, we are in a very different South Africa. The post-apartheid honeymoon is definitively over. The very real and extraordinary achievements of having emerged from civil war and created a democratic polity and a relatively prosperous economy are in danger of being obscured. Daily life is dominated by fear of criminal attack. The government is racked by debilitating political infighting. Corruption and patronage politics are rife. Although there have been massive changes in the racial distribution of wealth, huge portions of the population remain locked in chronic poverty.

The generation I have been writing about have gone on to different fates. Many have emigrated, their energies exhausted. Some have become political hacks of various stripes. Quite a number have parleyed their political skills into economic self-advancement, becoming some of the new millionaires of the post-struggle economy; some of yesterday's impoverished and persecuted trade union organisers have become today's corporate board members. Some cling to the political dogmas of their youth in a way which no longer speaks to the present.

Yet a large number hang on to some sort of egalitarian vision and continue to work creatively in education, law, journalism, medicine, community organisation, theatre. They have made an enormous difference to the development of a democratic civil society in South Africa. That contribution is not necessarily appreciated by the new powers that be, who often seem to wish that they had a less vigorous civil society to deal with. But it is the more important for that.

How does this story look in retrospect?

Perhaps the heart of what I have been reflecting on is the odd juxtaposition in a generation's experience of the disparate cultures of rock and roll and of Marxism. Rock and roll culture provided an escape from the conformity of state, family, school and army. It prepared a generation to take up ideas which negated everything they had been brought up to pursue. Marxism provided an apparent answer to all the political dilemmas they then faced. If Marxism ultimately proved a poor guide to the ironies of history, it nevertheless generated enormous political energies which had significant creative, political and cultural results.

Of course the two cultures had major incompatibilities. The 'conversion' to Marxism was sometimes accompanied by a somewhat puritanical turn in people's lives. For some Marxists the Counterculture was no more than 'bourgeois' ideology. But this was an authoritarian response. Those who had come to the left through the route of youth culture, did often bring to it an enriching libertarianism and cultural creativity lacking in the old left.

South African Marxism did produce an enormous amount of extremely valuable historical and sociological work. What remains important is its starting point in recognition of, and horror at, social inequality. It is surely to the credit of Marxists that they were seized by the unbearable nature of the social conditions of apartheid South Africa. Marxism provided a useful intellectual framework for getting to grips with this. And poverty and the inability to overcome it is certainly still the central question of South African society, which gives that work a continuing relevance.

Yet it is surely now apparent that the political pre-scriptions of Marxism are inadequate. For all the validity of some of their criticisms of liberalism, Marxists have never generated an adequate theory of the political rights needed in a democratic society. We know too that Marxism has been all too ready to apolo-gise for grotesquely undemocratic regimes – not just in the case of Stalin in the past, but also in the cases of Mao's China, Pol Pot's Cambodia, Mengistu's Ethiopia, and, in our own time, Mugabe's Zimbabwe.

Probably the most salient issue for the rock and roll generation is the politics of race in post-apartheid cir-cumstances. One of the great liberating features of the struggle era was the attempt by both black and white activists and intellectuals to move beyond simplistic race-thinking. The emphasis on overcoming class in-equality was one way to deal with this. Another was in the nonracial ideas that were such a feature of the UDF in the 1980s. Of course, in the South African context this was always a tricky operation, and racial tensions constantly re-emerged. Nevertheless, the leadership of Nelson Mandela in the transition embodied a real attempt to produce a new politics of South Africanism. But subsequently, a re-racialisation of South African politics has taken place. Every political issue is posed in crudely racial terms. If I express a difference with gov-ernment on a particular state policy, government will not accept that my objection is genuinely because I dis-agree with that policy; I am liable to be told that I'm objecting because I'm white. And if a black person agrees with me it is apparently because he or she is a tool of the whites. This is clearly no way to run a demo-cratic debate. The fact is that I have no interest in being part of a white 'community'; if I put forward a view it's because I've thought about it not because I'm repre-senting an interest group. Somehow, for President Mbeki white ethnic nationalist groupings can be dealt with respectfully, but independent-minded white liberals and leftists are a problem. It is notable that Mbeki provided a totally undeserved tribute to the late un-lamented PW Botha, while liberals are endlessly dispar-aged. Also too often, the solution to ethnic divides is often framed in terms of a kind of hokey culturalism. One prominent intellectual recently suggested that white men learn to dance like Johnny Clegg in order to be more African. As I have a bad hip I am unlikely to do this. But the more serious problem with this position is that it does not accept the freedom of expression that is part of the basis of the South African constitution. There cannot be cultural tests for citizenship. Strongly put, the problem for me is that I want to be South African but the current political leadership seems to insist that I be white.

Nevertheless the optimism of the rock and roll gene-ration is still there. Many of those I've been writing about would now feel distant from the culture of their youth. Few now listen to Bob Dylan singing, 'The answer is blowing in the wind.'

But the wind is still blowing all the same.

Jon Hyslop is deputy director of WISER and the author, most recently, of *The Notorious Syndicalist*.

Why Am I Here?

Achille Mbembe

Translated from French by Maureen Anderson

I arrived in South Africa after having travelled the distance of the Atlantic Triangle – from Africa to Europe, from Europe to the New World, and from the New World to West Africa initially and then to the southern hemisphere. Many African intellectuals dream about the Old World. I made exactly the opposite choice.

It is true that I continue to teach regularly in several American universities. But South Africa is now my centre of gravity. That fact that my wife is white and that my daughter, *métisse*, has South African citizenship – all this is not without consequence in how I try to think and live, or what I make of my position here. I am not a South African citizen. Though I have a permanent contract at an academic institution in Johannesburg, I only have – at least for the moment – the status of temporary resident in this country. Having kept my birth nationality – I am Cameroonian – I am required every three years to renew my residency permit. I define myself as an Afropolitan citizen – someone who, keeping a centre of gravity in Africa (and not necessarily where one was born), retains the possibility of circulating through the world, in the context of his profession.

But it is not enough to arrive somewhere and settle in. One must still make sense of that place. In my case, I started out as a regular visitor and ended up becoming a relative. But despite having become a relative, my way of seeing the South African experiment remains, in many ways, that of a close outsider. This conjunction of distance and proximity explains the impertinence of some of my observations. It also explains the attachment I feel towards this country. Because of my wife and my daughter, I can no longer separate out my fate from that of South Africa. Being here, but not being from here, I cannot claim to speak in the name of anybody – certainly not for South Africans themselves. And I give the country great credit for never having requested that, in order to live here, I silence myself or ask for an authorisation before I can speak.

I don't know if I will end my days here. How could I ever know this for sure? The fact is that I will have spent most of my adult life traversing the world, from one city to the next, following the whims of demand and accident, but also of choice. Born in the wake of the independence era, I am, in large part, the product of the first age of postcolonialism – its childhood and adolescence. I grew up in Africa in the shadow of triumphant nationalism. In those days the national debt, structural adjustment programmes, pervasive unemployment, widespread corruption and crime, pillages and predatory wars, played little role in ordinary experience – certainly they did not have the same degree of intensity as they do today.

WHERE I GREW UP

After the Second World War, there emerged in the main urban centres of my country an anticolonialist movement that demanded immediate independence. Ideas of liberty, self-constitution and self-government swiftly spread to all layers of society, at least in the southern and western parts of the territory. As colonial repression intensified during the course of 1955, the independence movement was forced into an armed struggle for which it was hardly prepared. It was defeated by France, which then used this victory to its advantage when, at the time of decolonisation, it handed its power over to its native collaborators.

Some of the leading figures of the struggle for independence were executed. Their mortal remains were dishonoured and hastily buried, as if they belonged to some small-time highway bandits. This was notably so with Ruben Um Nyobé, whose assassination prefigured so many others – Patrice Lumumba, Amilcar Cabral, Eduardo Mondlane – on that long list of African martyrs of independence. Those among them who took to the road of exile were, largely, hunted down and murdered, as was the case with Félix Moumié. Still others pursued armed struggle during the first decade of independence. They were all apprehended. Some of them, such as Osendé Afana, were beheaded. Others, like Ernest Ouandié, were the victims of a public execution following a judicial masquerade.

This armed struggle – initially against the colonial power but later assuming the form of a civil war after formal independence was declared – our government saddled with the term 'terrorism' in order to deny it any political signification. Thus it could declare a state of exception precisely to overcome the resistance by extra legal means. The names of the nationalist movement's principle protagonists were banned from public discourse in order to expunge from the nation's memory all events associated with the independence struggle. Long after their executions, it was forbidden to mention them in public, to refer to their teachings, or to have their writings in one's possession. Everything operated as if they had never existed, and as if their struggle had been no more than some banal criminal enterprise. In this way the newly independent state attempted to escape the injunction long ago delivered to Cain: 'Cain, where is your brother Abel?'

Conjoined to the birth of the independent state were thus the coffins and the skulls of those who had hurriedly been laid to rest, but denied a proper funeral. I think that if today I find myself so spiritually remote from my native country without ever ceasing to worry about it – without it ever ceasing to preoccupy me – it is in large part because of its refusal to recognise its birth at the edge of the grave.

This refusal to care for the fallen dead of the struggles for independence and self-determination – that primal act of cruelty against the 'brother' – all of this became, early on, not only the principal object of my intellectual life, but also the prism through which, I realise today, I developed my critique of Africa as a place that harbours the skull of the deceased family member.

By inaugurating its life among nations through a refusal to care for its own deceased relatives, my native

147

country did not just show its willingness to found a political order on the radical denial of the humanity of political adversaries. It also marked its preference for a politics of cruelty over a politics of fraternity and community. It sacrificed the idea of freedom born of struggle for an independence that the master, in his magnanimity, was kind enough concede to his slave.

Or at least, that is how things seem to me today. In my youth, the official discourse only spoke of 'order and discipline', 'self-centreed development', 'self-sufficiency', and 'peace and national unity.' There were various techniques to assimilate us to this *doxa*. For example, school children were required to sing the national anthem every morning. We learned to sing it with fervour, with rounded torso and clear tone, while facing the waving, tricoloured flag. We knew that other countries had their own flags. But ours, with its blazing green, red and yellow, was the only one that we really needed to honour. Every year the national holiday was celebrated with great patriotism. We would eagerly participate in the parade. It was understood that, when passing in front of the official platform, we would march in step like so many little soldiers, our banners held high, singing the praises of the potentate.

The fact is that, in our country, the nation and the potentate have always been one and the same. The potentate engendered the nation, and the nation was only sustained by the grace of its potentate. He was, all at once, the 'Father of the Nation', the 'Enlightened Leader', the 'Tireless Builder', the 'Great Helmsman', the 'Foremost Farmer' and the 'Foremost Sportsman'. 'One People, One Party, One Leader,' proclaimed the official slogan.

He had such a need to be loved, our potentate. And the entire populace, we loved him as much as possible. His image, for example, decorated every public space. Often it accompanied us into our private homes. Every large public place, every major intersection, every main avenue and boulevard, the national football stadium – anything that counted for anything in our country automatically carried his name. His face graced our national currency, seemingly bestowing it with a value it would scarcely have carried otherwise. On the eve of every presidential election, the 'Enlightened Guide' would receive, from all of the country's vital forces, countless 'motions of support'. Through this 'spontaneous' action, we would again implore him to become our sole election candidate. And every five years, at the conclusion of our single party's congress, in a strong voice he would declare, amidst the acclamations of the people: 'All right, I accept! I accept!'

He accepted so many times that, for more than twenty years, my generation only knew one party and one leader 'regularly elected' with results approaching 99 per cent of the vote.

Thus were we decolonised without truly being free. Independence without freedom, freedom endlessly postponed – such was, I later discovered, the unique hallmark of the postcolony, the true legacy of the travesty that was colonisation. Though it is not always recognised today, on the whole Africa did not, for all its years under colonialism, inherit very much. In my own country there was almost no heavy infrastructure. Two or three bridges built by the Germans. A few scattered schools, dispensaries and hospitals. Scarcely any roads, railroads or airfields. One or two seaports for exporting tropical products to the metropolis. No national museum. Not a single national theatre. Not a single university. A small elite.

No wonder our government never stopped reminding us that we were starting from practically nothing; that we were bound to build everything from scratch, and that we thus required peace, order and discipline. Indeed, we had our five-year plan – a true fairy tale. Every five years the 'Beloved Guide' took great care to tell us how many tons of cocoa, coffee, cotton, bananas, tea and palm oil the nation planned to harvest; how many kilometers of roads would be paved; how many factories would be built; how many children would be vaccinated; what the new school enrolment rate would be; how many new jobs would be created, and so forth.

We needed order, peace and discipline. As a result everything, or almost everything, had to be multiplied by one. This obsession with oneness – unity at all cost – was the rule. We were told we had no need for several political parties. One sufficed, otherwise 'tribal war' would ensue. Similarly with civic organisations, unions, the radio, the university, the media – one daily newspaper, each morning with the inset face of the 'Enlightened Guide' and a 'thought of the day' – an excerpt from one of his countless speeches. Any real or presumed dissidence was considered 'subversion'. And 'subversion' incurred the highest cost. We had our own Robben Islands – Mantoum and Tcholliré for instance, where many spent two or even three decades in total anonymity. Draconian laws dating from the colonial era allowed our government to 'nip in the bud' any attempt at rebellion. It was well understood: however much we were independent, we could not entirely decolonise at the same time.

I cannot say today how it was that, from this pathetic theatre of power, we managed to produce anything more than words. What I remember most from the immediate post-independence era is the *name* – the suddenly acquired power to say 'I'; the suddenly opened possibility of giving oneself a proper name when, before, our parents had been either without their own name or saddled with the name of others. We had a name to honour, ours – a name to which we would now need to give a face and a form. There was also a country to which we all belonged, and which belonged to us all. We would have to share it. This 'politics of sharing' was referred to by our government as the 'policy of regional equilibrium'. It was supposed to thwart the possibility of hegemony by any particular ethnic group. That was, in any case, the spirit of the times.

I thus belong to that generation of Africans that has never had any other name to honour but our own. The spirit of the times made us feel accountable to our common name. It may be hard to understand today, but this name played an enormous role in how we imagined our place in the world. Because we had a name of our own, we went out into the world without the least bit of shame. Instead we stood tall and sure of ourselves. For after all, in those days, at least in my native country, we did not depend on 'development aid'. In school curricula, we would read our own novelists alongside French literature. We would learn our history and our geography alongside the history and geography of the rest of the world. On the radio, we listened to our national music along with the rest of the world's music. At the table, we ate our own delicacies. No-one ever really dreamed of leaving the country for good. Some would leave to study abroad, but always with the firm intention of returning to work at home. Failure consisted of not being in a position to return to the native country. We did not have, at that time, a single illegal immigrant in any country in the world.

Unlike many South Africans, my generation grew up in an environment where the humanity of a black person was not even remotely called into question. We did not have to respond directly to the prejudice that deemed Blacks inferior beings, a people without history. I grew up knowing that such prejudice could only be generated by a sick and troubled mind. Having no direct experience of colonial rule, for a long while I did not understand what 'race' was about. We had always been governed by black Africans. There were some Whites who lived among us and worked in our country. But they could never act as though they were our masters and we never allowed them to act as if they were.

This is why South Africa represented, in the eyes of just about everyone, such a scandal.

I truly cannot recall a single week of my youth in which the government of my country did not issue a condemnation of the 'colonial, minority, fascist, racist and immoral regime of Pretoria'.

Granted, when it came to immoral regimes there were certainly others. The 'fascist' version of Portuguese colonialism in Angola, Guinea-Bissau and Mozambique, Ian Smith's 'racist and minority' regime in Zimbabwe – our government taught us to despise them all. But the most visceral loathing, the most implacable hate, we were expected to reserve that for the 'colonial, minority, fascist, racist and immoral regime of Pretoria'. Thus it was that South Africa in general and Pretoria in particular were the consummate political Sodom and Gomorrah of my youth – places of moral corruption and utmost abjection.

It was thought that what was happening in that country was intrinsically perverse, profoundly vile, thoroughly obscene. We were convinced that what took place there constituted a terrible injury to human dignity and that no human language was adequate to condemn it. My generation grew up – or at any rate I did – in the shadow of this map of the world where South Africa represented, from start to finish, the absolute mark of infamy. One can understand how, under these conditions, the theme of 'the continent's complete liberation from colonialism and racism' had such resonance and so profoundly marked our imagination.

I LEFT MY COUNTRY EARLY ON

And yet I left my country early on, and I have never returned – at least not to live and work.

I did not hate my country. But I always had an uncomfortable relationship with the country where I was born. For instance, I did not know how to speak the street language without which one could not gain full membership into one's age group. I was incapable of the proper machismo, which required a constant strutting in front of the girls; or, when among the guys, argu-ing endlessly about who among you possessed the hard-est and most well-endowed cock. Then there was all the bluster – coming to blows over nothing, in a flash, just to be seen; or chasing after trivialities like clothing style, the taste for blinding colours or shiny shoes. I was awk-ward at everything that required any use of the hands. Manual work was hard for me. Traditional African music always pulled me into a trance, like others who smoked hashish. In my mind, it was the language of a tragedy the name of which I couldn't grasp. But despite this power, I was incapable of dancing 'African style', with its lubricity and endless contortions, the body entirely floating and limb-free. I would always attract sarcastic comments: 'Oh, does he ever dance like a white guy!'

Having been educated in a Catholic school, I found it insurmountably difficult to reconcile myself to aspects of political society and official culture that struck me, even then, as so excessive: the centrality of the phallus in the process of symbolising life, power and pleasure; the idea according to which to be a 'chief' is to indulge in utter excess without reserve or hindrance; the widespread deference to fetishes; sor-cery beliefs that tended to make humans forever the playthings of forces beyond them; the propensity to for-get so much, the incapacity to generate a collective memory and the disdain attached to the very idea of the future, to say nothing of the dead; a certain native spirit of materialism, particularly destructive because it flowed directly from the principle of unrestrained, radical expenditure rather than production; the oscillation between compassion on one side and proclivities towards cruelty, the spectacle and excess on the other.

But I also lived in a society that showed other attributes: an unfathomable sense of compassion, conviviality and frugality; endurance in the face of any hardship, and the capacity to make the best of very little; the extraordinary strength of familial forms of solidarity; the virtues of openness and hospitality; all those small acts of everyday life that showed the degree to which people were ready to take care of each other in their normal communities; the vitality of intellectual reflection, and that kind of pride and natural self-respect that reflected a self-presence that colonialism was never able to destroy.

Leaving allowed me to gain some distance on the contradictions and logics described above. I had left – by pure coincidence – in the same month in which our 'Beloved Guide' finally decided to step down.

I completed my university studies in Paris, like others who go off to Oxford and Cambridge. I arrived in a city that had successfully pushed the working population from the centre towards the extremities. The deprived classes – among whom there was a sizable number from the former colonies – formed an immense cordon around the well off. This was a city where the art of utopian thought was still alive to a certain extent – the culture of strikes and insurrection too. Cafés were still major centres of sociality and conversation. The intellectual world and cultural life were still dominated by powerful figures such as Michel Foucault, Jacques Derrida, Pierre Bourdieu, Claude Lévi-Strauss, Fernand Braudel, Simone de Beauvoir,

Raymond Aron. Rich or poor, Parisians still knew how to pursue their pleasures. This was a very competitive city where the arts were vibrant, achievements were celebrated and every mark of distinction counted.

Through close contact with people, travel and, above all, reading, I discovered France, an old country that was so aware of its history – which it tended to glorify constantly – and so jealous of its traditions. My Parisian years also allowed me to see that behind every established culture – and especially the established colonial cultures – there is always a nocturnal side hiding behind a mask of reason and civility. France's nocturnal side – I was aware of it even before I arrived. At the time of my country's struggles for independence and self-determination, had France not played a prominent role in refusing burial for, and bringing about the banishment of, the dead? Did its Africa policy not thoroughly demonstrate that to grant formal independence to former colonies is one thing and for the former colonial empire to truly de-colonise itself is another? Did its tradition of abstract universalism not paradoxically contradict its faith in the republican dogma of universal equality?

Where Paris and France were concerned, I thus always considered myself a foreigner, or to be precise, someone on the way to some place else, a passer-by. But at the same time, by virtue of acculturation into the country's language, tastes and mores, and by socialisation into major aspects of its literary and academic culture I ended up becoming an inhabitant – an heir. Whole archives of knowledge and human thought were opened to me. I devoured them to such a point that today, I conceive of myself as a legitimate claimant to its heritage. Did Fanon not say that we would inherit the entire world?

I arrived in New York after my doctorate to take up a teaching position in an Ivy League university. New York is not just the metropolis that marked my entry into the United States. It is also the place where I began, for the first time, to develop a sense of the global world – the global ecumene. It was in New York that I was able, for the first time, to contemplate concretely the face of the universal as celebrated by the Senegalese poet LS Senghor. I spent hours walking in Central Park as well as in old ethnic neighborhoods, including some areas with large concentrations of Blacks. I took taxi-cabs and the subway and walked from home to work. I went to restaurants in 'global' neighbourhoods in which diverse native-born minority groups lived side by side with new immigrants of different national origins.

Only in New York did I realise how the French version of universality expressed itself in a language that was, in the end, quite narcissistic, monocoloured and provincial. In New York, for the first time I discovered a metropolis founded on a simple idea – the idea of hospitality – and a contradiction – segregation along the 'colour line'. Large numbers of southern and eastern European immigrants (including Italians, Greeks, Russians, Austrians, Romanian Jews) had come here in the late nineteenth and early twentieth centuries. English, Irish and German immigrants had arrived earlier. African-Americans had been here until the draft riots of 1863 when working-class Irish rampaged through their small neighbourhoods, forcing them to flee to the city of Brooklyn. They started coming back around the

1860s, mostly from the South; then in large numbers in the 1910s, with an influx from the West Indies. By that time, Harlem was well on its way to becoming the capital of global black modernity. During my time in New York, I would go to Harlem to buy black radical literature and black music, to listen to street preachers or to watch a musical performance. Indeed, it is at the Apollo Theatre in Harlem that I first saw a performance by Fela Anikulapo-Kuti.

By the time I arrived in New York, a sizable proportion of African-Americans still lived in highly segregated, inner-city ghettos although many had moved to African-American concentrated residential settings in the suburbs. Nevertheless, here was an extraordinary juxtaposition of cultures that made the city a quintessential metropolis of optimism, of faith in oneself and in what was yet to come. In this city, something new was always being created. Everything here seemed to lead to new beginnings – the swarms of peoples, ethnicities and humanities, the cacophony of voices, the mixing of colours and sounds, black music, a black intelligentsia. Here I encountered, far more than in Paris, an African counterpart in the African-American – an African presence at the birth of modernity on the one hand and on the other hand the figure of the slave, an insurrectional sign that, in its radicality, was a constant reminder that where freedom is concerned there are only claimants *ayant droits.*

Seeing it up close, this is what made New York more than a city – an Idea. I have to say that, as an Idea, or as a movement of the mind, New York literally seduced me. I was profoundly stimulated in my intellectual work and the city became a highly creative and reflective medium. For the first time in my life I could distinctly hear the clamouring of worlds, the rustling echoes of that juxtaposition of nations, races and ethnicities which, once again, Senghor had spoken of. I, too, wanted to be a full participant in that epiphany. That said, do I need to specify that I have not forgotten that New York is also one of the most segregated metropolitan areas with respect to African-Americans or Blacks in the United States? In this same metropolis, Amadou Diallo could be riddled with 40 bullets by police for happening to be at the wrong place at the wrong time – a much more commonplace event among people of his type? And that, for hundreds of thousands of slave descendants in the New World, the prison soon replaced the plantation?

I taught for several years in the United States before returning to Africa as an adult. For four years I served, in Dakar, Senegal, as the executive director of an organisation whose official mission was to promote social science research on the continent. It was the most frustrating experience of my entire life. Perhaps that is why this city at the crossroads, bordering the Sahel and the Atlantic, and steps away from the Old Continent and the New World, remained mute in my soul. I enjoyed its vibe, its music (*mbalax*) to which I did not know how to dance, the dust that came in from the desert when the harmattan winds blew, and my seaside house near my illustrious neighbour, the filmmaker and novelist, Ousmane Sembène. I was fond of Dakar, but it would only be a point of transit for me.

CAPE TOWN INTERLUDE

I left Dakar knowing that, where Africa was concerned, it was better to plunge in with eyes wide open. I could have returned to France or the United States and pursued the experiences of universality that Paris and New York had hinted at. Instead I found myself in one of the strangest cities in Africa, Cape Town.

Thus I did not come to South Africa in the manner of those from an earlier era who disembarked in Tanzania in search of 'African Socialism'. Nor did I arrive in search of employment. I came in several stages, so to speak, without knowing that I would remain. It was enough for me to just share that period of my life with a South African academic whom I had fallen in love with while in Dakar and who would later become my wife – to my utmost delight. When I first arrived I knew almost nothing about South Africa, apart from what my government had previously taught me. Various stereotypical images could be added to that: the struggle against apartheid, Nelson Mandela, Soweto, and so on. I was not even familiar with the Truth and Reconciliation Commission. One vague philosophical idea nevertheless animated me: the question of *interruption*. I was deeply intrigued by the event by which a society formerly at war with itself had consciously chosen to escape the deadly logic of repetition and decided to start anew, renegotiating in the process the terms and conditions of its existence among nations. That this profoundly ethical and political gesture had taken place in the most powerful, intricate and complex country in Africa only added to my intellectual curiosity.

Still not knowing whether I was here to stay, I was content for almost two years to passively absorb everything my senses encountered. Literally before my eyes, I beheld a fractured country, beset by the mark of the Beast, the god with a goat's hindquarters *le dieu-au-cul-de-chèvre* – the ideology of white supremacy that many had worshipped here for decades, if not centuries. I quickly realised that something truly abject had taken place here and that it had incited an equally fierce resistance – in fact one of the noblest struggles for human freedom in modern history. One could still see the marks of the Beast in the landscape, the architecture, street names, statues and monuments, ways of speaking, the countless oddities of everyday life – for instance when one found oneself the only black in a restaurant in a so-called African city; or, going to a shop, one witnessed at first hand the hierarchical logics of yesterday: the White giving orders, the Coloured at the counter, and the Black at the bottom, lifting heavy loads, cleaning and smiling at the countless petty humiliations he or she has to endure in order to make a living.

In Cape Town, my morning ritual consisted of reading newspapers and listening to radio talk shows. I couldn't but notice the extreme force and intensity with which the question of the 'original guilt' – the cruel incision racism had been and was still, to a certain extent – was still posed. It looked to me as if the deepest marks were the mental scarifications that could be sensed throughout, among Blacks and Whites, Coloureds and Indians – including those who claimed to have escaped unscathed from the insanity. It was clear that in the maelstrom that was apartheid – and before that, through centuries of colonial paternalism and phalloc-racy – everyone had lost, to varying degrees, more than a bit of decency. Here, evil had found a tongue. Despite the thousand little compassionate gestures carried out from day to day, in the relations between masters and servants, in the churches where Blacks and Whites used to worship the same God separately, in the resistance movement and interracial friendships made fragile by material inequalities and the repressive context, an opaque wall of ignorance had been erected and it had prevented any true sense of proximity, reciprocity or similarity. Although depending on each other for their daily existence, Blacks and Whites were cut off from all human closeness, so much so that the biggest obstacle to the project of nonracialism was the difficulty – expe-rienced both by Blacks and Whites – of seeing in the other the face of a fellow human, or of merely imagin-ing what it would mean to be in the other's place; to have, somewhere, any commonality.

It was precisely this idea of commonality that the ide-ology and practice of racial segregation had tried to kill. One could see everywhere the injuries and heaps of refuse resulting from that attempt to murder an Idea. The country was littered with remains – that mix-ture of stupefying beauty and ugliness so characteristic of places where the demon had, at a given moment, chosen to dwell.

I spent a great deal of time listening to people's statements and observing their behaviour in public places – in restaurants, at the bank, in shops, cafés, stores and other public places. Sometimes it seemed as if they had just been released from an asylum or a penal colony. Some of them no longer knew where they had been throughout those obscene years. There was a very ancient guilt they wanted to forget because it was giving rise to strange emotional events. Others had no desire to know anything. Not even the name of the place they currently inhabited – and even less who their new rulers were. They continually told themselves stories – they lived here still, but were convinced they truly belonged to an 'elsewhere' an entire people tried to reproduce here, almost without change, like the former English colonists on the banks of the Potomac. Others, with political power having been taken from them, were caught in an infinite state of grief, melancholia and sorrow. They were lamenting and dreaming about the return to the bygone years when the worship of the golden calf – racial supremacy – was the rule. The Adamic state of innocent racism, when the law precluded any sense of guilt, and no touch of scandal was assigned to hate – all of this was now but an empty picture frame, the insolvency of the debtor's soul. Still others were willing to look to the future, but hardly knew how to locate themselves in relation to the present. Others wanted to carry on as if nothing had changed, as if everything had stayed the same. They tried to convince themselves that they, too, had stayed the same. Only time had fled, passing above their heads, almost without their knowledge.

More than once, I felt as if I had found myself in some funeral casino. The contrast between the opulence of some and the chronic sickness, premature death and extraordinary misery of others was so utterly astounding. The contrast was apparent from the first entry into the city. I had lived in many countries, but never had I been so inclined to pour hand-outs to passers-by than in South Africa. Here was a society whose founding violence had always been material inequality. It was as if the gradual consumption of the life of the poorest served as the kindling to the plentitude of the wealthy.

One of the questions I could not stop wondering about had to do with the shameful colonial wounds which stare you in the face, make you bleed long after the event, a perpetual witness to the obscenity of times past – the names of the streets, public places, avenues and boulevards, mountains, lakes, gardens, dams, monuments and museums. Should these signs be seen as symbols of the mental expatriation from which every form of racism and colonial mimicry sustains itself? Why so much resistance to creating and inventing for oneself? Why had almost all of them been left in place after apartheid? Why had they not been rounded up, all of these iron or clay-mounted statues, all these monuments and signs of racial insanity, and put in a park or a museum?

But I was interested in more than post-apartheid delirium, or the complicated story of exactly what was repressed, destroyed or coopted. Right from the beginning, I wanted to lift the veil enough to glimpse the complex history that lay behind it, its paradoxes and its potentialities. The South Africa in which I found myself seemed to be a society made up of countless drawers. I was struck by the extent to which, here, capitalist forms of accumulation had reached deep in the society, and the prominent place given to structures of private property and to the legal regimes set up to ensure their permanence. I also noticed the extent to which the country was woven by a multiplicity of heritages and political cultures – from the remnants of colonial liberalism in the main urban agglomerations to the deep-rooted rural paternalism in the farms; from the residues of the racist obscurantism that had always existed – of which apartheid was but the extreme manifestation – to the populism inherited from the lumpen-politics of the years of resistance; and from the melange of corruption, brutality and despotism of the years of the National Party and the Bantustans to the veneer of a cosmopolitan and transnational culture that has never been able to define itself as such.

There were also, more than elsewhere in the continent, the trappings of modernity – a relatively dense network of industries and services, a functional urban infrastructure, good roads, airports and postal services, luxurious hotels clean and spacious, countless malls, those temples to commodities that are the substitute for public space, their stalls crammed with almost everything, and rich people who shop until they drop, especially during the end-of-year festive season. There were shiny new cars speeding along the highways before disappearing under the trees, behind the electric fences and walls on which the famous sign was unfailingly posted: 'Armed Response'. Then there was an exceedingly large canine population, with breeds specially trained to put Blacks back in their place – or so everyone told me.

And then there were some rudiments of a liberal society – four or five universities worthy of the name; an intelligentsia disoriented in the aftermath of the democratic transition and now slowly reconstituting itself; a relatively free and privately owned press of distressing intellectual mediocrity; theatres, galleries and museums – if poorly financed; a cohort of nongovernmental organisations; a relatively autonomous cultural sphere, yet with very little support; a population which barely reads; the basic foundations of the rule of law; a relative degree of sophistication among the best of the elites and, above all, an enormous potential that only asked to be exploited.

The other drawer was that of personal life. Paradoxically, Cape Town was also the place where I rediscovered private happiness, not unlike the joys I had known during my years of innocent childhood in my own country. I had always lived my academic life as a kind of priesthood. In this beautiful-ugly space, I was discovering the possibility of a different kind of relationship between the sphere of work and the protective sphere of the family, an inner life and an inner freedom that needed to be nurtured once again. The people I shared my life with (my wife-to-be, her family, and a few friends) introduced me to some of what lay beneath the surface of this place and its chronic disaster zones. Alongside immense possibilities of harming, alternative modes of relating had been developed. To a large extent, the struggle to overcome indifference and blindness had been relentless. Moral sensibility had not been totally eroded. While caring for themselves, some people were still capable of caring for others. After all, the basis for a new human communality was there.

Such were my first impressions after almost two and

a half years of immersion. A year after having left Dakar for good, I was recruited by a new research institute based at the University of the Witwatersrand, one with a powerful and evocative acronym – WISER – the Wits Institute for Social and Economic Research. Never before had I found myself in such a congenial academic space. The director of this new institute had conceived of it as a space for creative freedom and intellectual friendship. The institute had as its mission to reflect upon the transformations taking place in South Africa after apartheid. And that is how I found myself in Johannesburg. It was only having left the Cape and after we had settled in Johannesburg that this country really started to become an object of political and intellectual interrogation for me. That was when I began to consciously observe it and to study its history.

JOHANNESBURG AND THE IDEA OF SOUTH AFRICA
It was then that I discovered an African country the very Africanness of which followed from its transnationality. Here, in effect, is what distinguishes South Africa from other African nations – the fact that from an empirical point of view, this nation is, strictly speaking, a *diasporic nation*, a meeting of nations, accidental and brutal to be sure, but a meeting nevertheless. The country's successive regimes long tried to efface that Africanness. At times they dreamed of making South Africa an English county and, at other times, the Holy Land for a particular ethnic group foolish enough to believe in its election by God and, in so doing, willing to wear the mask of death and to set in motion an incalculable violence – a force for harm, carelessness and neglect. Indeed, the

concept of racial supremacy, long dominant in South African life, was not just the very antithesis of liberty. It was the manifestation of a malady of the mind – racism. As was to be expected, this denial of liberty and rights for the majority, all in the name of the survival of a single race, fed its social struggles. These social struggles were modern from start to finish because their central stake was freedom.

For me the place that stands for South Africa's deepest potential, in the eyes of the world at any rate, is first and foremost Johannesburg. Just as Paris was my window onto a way of thinking, and New York my watchtower onto the global world, so the South Africa of my political and intellectual reflection is, above all, Johannesburg. Historically, this city was built by people who by and large came from elsewhere (*uitlanders*) – whether from overseas or from other regions of South Africa and southern Africa. Today still, many continue to arrive from elsewhere. Johannesburg has the potential to become the equivalent of New York on an African scale – a place of sedimentation of the world's cultures and the richness carried by each of them. But the city must first conceive of itself in this way, and make this its project.

In Johannesburg, I saw the premier industrial metropolis in the continent. Unlike Cape Town, I also saw a city that boldly claimed its Africanness. Here, black people were not relegated to the margins. They inhabited the centre of the city. Here, I could see a range of possible lives for Blacks that were not limited to the dialectics of cruelty and misery I had witnessed elsewhere.

I also saw a city that had witnessed the most decisive and intense struggles, ones that changed the face of

South Africa. These struggles involved the definition of the terms of political belonging. But they were also about the definition of the terms of property and possession, of *ownership* and economic citizenship. At stake in this twofold struggle was, as I have said, the constitution of a *'universal nation'* because, coming from everywhere, its inhabitants formed not only a world within a world, but were called upon, as Fanon would say, to become heirs to the world in its entirety.

The abolition of apartheid did not put an end to these struggles. It simply shifted their terms. If South Africa effectively belongs to all who live here, then one can no longer be defined by race, and the latter should no longer carry any privilege. But this would also mean that privileges previously accumulated precisely on the basis of race must be shared and extended to everyone. This is what is meant by deracialisation. In order for those who, for centuries on end, benefited from the privileges of race to legitimately claim rights of citizenship in this new nation where race no longer counts, they must subscribe to a new ethic of sharing and conviviality.

The greatest possible liberty for all will only be obtained when many if not all have something to lose. Thus there can be no commitment to liberty that is not accompanied by an equal commitment to justice, redress and equality. One cannot leave to market forces alone the task of spearheading the triple undertaking of liberty, justice and equality. For it is an intrinsically political undertaking. But it is also a cultural undertaking. This is why the post-apartheid state errs in granting so little weight to the arts and the humanities in the project of transforming this society.

To become a 'universal nation' – such is South Africa's Idea, its call in the history of our modernity. But for the moment, South Africa is not conscious of its Idea. This country has not yet awakened to its Idea. For it is still encumbered by the burdens of its countless wounds. It is still rife with the violence inscribed in its social structures – the question of food, sleep, health, schooling and shelter. A terrible load is still placed on the shoulders of the poor. It is still too easy to die for no reason in contemporary South Africa. There is still too much talk of rights and not enough of responsibility. Far too many of its citizens still have nothing to lose. Its elites, black and white, are too consumed by greed and the pursuit of wealth. Too many excuses are still manufactured for its too high levels of crime, corruption and illiteracy. Its society remains, in many respects, a society of one-way corridors, with too few crossroads, too few points of contact and bifurcation. It needs to set itself free from the prison of 'race'. Threatened by the spirit of commercialism and the cult of instrumental reason, it must revive the creative forces of the mind and revalorise artistic and cultural creation to its full worth.

In spite of these shortcomings, South Africa will remain the centre of gravity for my intellectual work as long as I keep seeing in its past and present the unique possibility, in the history of African modernity, of a country that might become the first truly universal nation.

Achille Mbembe is a senior researcher at WISER. He is the author, most recently, of *On the Postcolony*, which won the 2006 Bill Venter/Altron Literary Award.

Losing My Mind

Justice Malala

i

I know exactly when I went insane. It was on 1 December 2006.

I was short with my sister and my daughter. I screamed at my wife. I checked the locks on the house. Twice. I screamed at my wife again because there were no shutters on the windows.

The burglar alarm went off twice in the night. I lay awake, hearing noises and footsteps and imagining monsters at the door. The next day, my sister asked if I was okay. I asked why, and she said I had a wild look in my eye.

We were moving back into our house in Parkview, probably the most beautiful suburb in Johannesburg, after living in a flat nearby for five months while our house was being renovated.

My wife, now eight months pregnant with our second child, had managed the renovations. I loved living in the flat. She hated it, and wanted to move back into our renovated house as quickly as possible. For her, it was five months in the flat and no more; it was 1 December or nothing.

It rained on 1 December. Someone called me and wished me Happy World AIDS Day.

The movers did not arrive at 10 am as scheduled. After threatening phone calls by my wife and just wait-ing, waiting, waiting they arrived at 4 pm.

They were shoddy, but quick. We left the flat an hour later. As they unloaded the truck, I became obsessed with knowing where all our keys were. I asked my wife, Justine, constantly, to make sure the workers did not go into the bedrooms. Everything was just piled into the living room for us to sort out. This is what I wanted, despite every box being marked to show where it should go.

A guy who was handing down the boxes from the truck was looking at my wife, looking at our house, at the premises. In my mind, I started thinking that he was casing us out. When he came over to me and asked if he could have some water, he was, it seemed, confirm-ing all my worst suspicions.

That night, when they had left, all I could see was his face at the window, a gun in his hand.

Four months later, as I write this, I still see his face at the window, a gun in his hand. Sometimes it is diffe-rent. Sometimes he is putting my daughter in the oven and threatening to turn it on if I do not tell him where the safe is. Sometimes I am shooting him.

These things do not belong in a book. This is stuff for a therapy session. But I have been there, and it has not worked.

ii

At exactly 10 pm on 6 February 2006, my wife and I are making love in our bed. My wife sees a man at the win-dow pointing a gun at us. She screams. I dive down.

He shoots at me and misses. My wife is running out the door. He shoots at her. He misses.

'You have to take back your space,' says Kim, our trauma therapist. 'You have to make that space feel like it is yours again.'

The bullet holes remain in our walls for months.

The guard we have hired, with his panic button and a knobkerrie, sits outside reading the Bible and nodding off. Every time we go out and come back late, he is so fast asleep he does not hear us arrive.

We go on holiday to England and France four months later.

I sleep, for the first time, like I have not slept in months.

When we return to South Africa everything is in place: we have rented a flat in nearby Killarney, the builders start demolishing one part of the house. For two days, we have only one wall between us and the outside world.

It is winter. It is cold and the wind howls like a wolf in the night. For two nights I blame my wife for everything. I blame her for not making sure we do not have to come back here. I hear noises in the night and jump up; she asks what's wrong and I fume at her.

On the second night we lose the key to the door. There are workers everywhere. I blame her. I am totally unreasonable. I think one of them will attack us in the night. I do not sleep.

We move to the flat. There is underground parking. There is a guard, all day and night, at the door. I am not afraid.

I sleep like a baby.

I am happy.

One day I drive out of my garage and there are young black men fixing a Volkswagen Golf GTI in the underground parking. A while back, when we were still living in the house, I would have thought they had stolen it.

But I am not afraid. In the flat. In the building. On the second floor. Away from my own house, away from home.

iii

I am writing this for myself, perhaps to understand what has happened to me and my people. I am constantly afraid, so very afraid, of everyone and of everything.

I walk around and there is this fear. This fear that my phone will ring and my child will have been attacked. This fear that something will happen to my family. This fear that in the night there will be someone with a gun at my bedside.

It has happened to so many people I know.

My friend Mondli says he was up reading one night when he felt like going outside in his garden and sitting on his son Tongo's swing. But he did not.

'I was too afraid to go out into my own garden,' he says.

I am writing this because I am trying to understand why there are so many brutalised people around me; and why we are so quiet.

We say we are patriots.

iv

I do not know anyone who has left South Africa because of crime. Of course, I know people who have left and cite crime as a reason. I lived in London for three years and they were all over the place.

But I did not know them. They were white strangers. Their language was always laced with a certain anger that had nothing to do with crime, I believed. They were angry at affirmative action; they were angry at black economic empowerment.

But I felt a deep sense of loss in their anger. They were angry because they felt powerless; absolutely, truly, powerless.

I feel that way now about crime. Impotent. I feel weak in my legs and my arms.

v

My friends David and Sandra Rothschild are moving to London. They have been offered fabulous jobs there. They cannot say no.

The party is at Fino, a restaurant we love and which I reviewed for my first restaurant column in the *Financial Mail.*

In many ways, my column is a celebration of wealth. It is about people who eat oysters and who have an interest in food. I mix politics with food, but no-one reads the politics.

Politics is so yesterday. No-one cares. We are free now.

I find that black people read my column. When I started, I thought I would be addressing a black audience in the *Sowetan* and a white audience in the *Financial Mail.* But it is class, really, not race. The wealthy and educated read the *Financial Mail,* and the wealthy and educated black classes read the *Financial*

Mail for more than just the company news. They want food, drink and all sorts of other things. Style, perhaps. A pointer to what's hot and what's cool.

It is good to be black and educated in South Africa. If the fruits of freedom accrue to anyone, it is us. We might not be wealthy, but there is an expression that the politicians like using: 'We are taking our rightful place in the economic life of the country.'

We are middle-class.

They read my restaurant column.

We are at Sandra and David's party when a man accosts my wife. Without greeting, he bursts out: 'I understand that Peter and Justine are leaving because of you. What happened?'

My wife wants to belt him.

vi

Peter and Justine are leaving the country. They are the first people I am close to who are leaving because of crime.

Chillingly, it was the incident that took place at my house that turned them outwards, to other shores.

I use the word 'outwards' deliberately. To look outwards denotes to turn your back on what is inside, what is troubling. I always described myself as outward-looking; as being unconstrained by where I am and where I come from; as being open to the influences of the outside world.

I am shocked, one day, to find myself thinking of the word as being negative.

At once I know and I don't know how I feel about Peter and Justine leaving. I feel a deep loss. I feel a deep empathy with them. Yet I feel dazed; shell-shocked. The truth is that I feel as though I am being judged even though I fully understand why they are leaving. I feel that Justine and Peter have found us wanting.

JM Coetzee, our Nobel laureate in literature who recently received Australian citizenship, said: 'Leaving a country is, in some respects, like the break-up of a marriage. It is an intimate matter.'

The point about all those South Africans I met in London and other parts of the world complaining about South Africa was that I could put them in a box. They were everything from unreconstructed racists to people who needed, desperately, to justify their decision to leave.

But now? Well, now.

Peter and Justine are not South African. He is from New Zealand and she is Irish. They chose to come here: they love it here. I know. I have supped at their table, played with their children, shared books and all sorts of things with them.

Now they are leaving.

Coetzee is right. It feels like the worst of break-ups, when you are still in love with the partner that you are leaving.

vii

It is close.

They put a gun in Tony's mouth and make him beg. Then they take his car. They shoot David and take a cellphone. Martin squats and watches as they clear out the gym. He only remembers the gun to his head. They rape Lulu. Many times. Donny's shop is broken into every day. A schoolmate is shot on her way to work for her cellphone. She dies. She leaves two kids.

There is a man standing at Tom's mother's window. He is back the next day. She moves out. They live eight houses down from us.

Her husband is away on a business trip. That weekend I am away, too.

My wife does not tell me until I come back. I am afraid.

viii

I lock the doors. I put on the beams that now surround the house.

The hadedahs which have been a feature of the house for four years arrive at 4.30 am and set off the alarm linked to the beams. I jump out of my skin. I call ADT, the security firm.

It goes off again at 7 am. The ADT security guard looks at me as though I am demented when I ask him to walk around and ensure that everything is fine.

In the day, I check that the electric fence is working properly.

I call my mother three times. I am fine, she says.

ix

It is close.

In the *Sowetan* of 19 February, I write:

If you believe in God, I ask you to pray for the soul of Thato Radebe. This child, this flower still blooming, was brutally murdered two weeks ago.

Her body was found in open veld in Emdeni, Soweto, by a passerby.

178

There were bottles, condoms and sticks around her lifeless body. She had not just been murdered; she had been raped and brutalised in unimaginable ways.

She was 14 years old.

On the Sunday morning after she was found I spoke to *Sowetan* editor Thabo Leshilo.

'I cannot even begin to tell you about the horrific pictures we have here. I feel like vomiting. These criminals are destroying our country,' he said.

So the next day I did not read the story of how she died.

I avoided all the stories about Thato Radebe. What Leshilo had told me was too horrific.

Last week I called a company which I sometimes deal with and asked for the sales executive I had dealt with in the past. I was told she was off.

I went there to deliver some paperwork a few days later and the sales executive's colleague told me the reason Happy Radebe was not at work was because her daughter had been murdered.

That is when I realised that I knew Thato's mother, that this was not a murder that far removed from me.

I do not know what a parent feels like when they lose their child. I do not know how a parent continues to exist after going through what the parents and relatives of this child are going through now.

When I spoke to Leshilo two weeks ago I could feel the emotion in his voice. I could feel his pain and anger.

It was so powerful that I knew what he had seen in those pictures was barbaric.

So then, how do the parents and relatives of that child feel?

I had to stop my car and close my eyes for a while just thinking about Happy Radebe, the mother of that child. What does her pain feel like, I wondered? How could anyone inflict such horror and pain on a fellow human being? ...

[Steve] Biko once said: 'It becomes more necessary to see the truth if you realise that the only vehicle for change are these people who have lost their personality. The first step is to make the black man come to himself; to pump back life into his empty shell; to infuse him with pride and dignity; to remind him of his complicity in the crime of allowing himself to be misused and therefore letting evil reign supreme in the country of his birth.'

X

Thabo Mbeki, President, Republic of South Africa, 16 March 2007:

[T]he fact of the matter is that we still have a significant proportion of people among the white minority, but by no means everybody who is white, that continues to live in fear of the black, and especially African majority. For this section of our population, that does not 'find it too difficult to revert to the accustomed world of fear of the future', every reported incident of crime communicates the frightening and expected message that – the kaffirs are coming!

The colleague in government to whom I referred, Mr A, posed the rhetorical question – why are the Whites so determined to frighten themselves! The answer of course is that they have taken no such decision. Rather, the problem is that entrenched racism dictates that justification must be found for the persisting white fears of '*die swart gevaar*'.

xi

When I leave home, I first open the garage door, walk out onto the street and check that there is no-one there. When I return home, I drive around the block to check that there isn't anyone lurking about.

'Why are you doing black economic empowerment deals now?' I ask my friend Vuyo.

'Because a time will come when my children will ask me: "Dad, what were you doing when all the educated black people were making millions through BEE?"'

I am at a party when talk turns to Peter and Justine's imminent departure.

'Nothing has happened to them. I don't know why they are leaving,' says one man.

'Should they wait to be shot or raped?' asks another.

It is very quiet.

xii

Our neighbour is American, single. I have never met her. She is moving out to a flat because she no longer feels safe in the suburb. Our houses are a block down from the Parkview police station.

I hear an alarm going off. All I can think to do is turn the beams around my house on and close the windows. I lock the doors.

A minute later my wife comes to the living room. 'I thought I heard a scream. Maybe you should go and check.'

I go out of the gate and press the buzzer to the

house next door. Our neighbour has been attacked. As she comes to the house for the second-last time, two men follow her into the yard, hold a gun to her head and tell her not to scream. They take a laptop, keys and a wallet.

A car is waiting for them at the gate. They make a quick getaway.

'I begged them not to take my passport. Thank God they did not take it,' she says.

Even at times like these, we are a nation that is grateful for small mercies.

xiii

My neighbour's other neighbour, a strapping, fresh-faced young man who regularly runs round the lake where I run, arrives on the scene with his girlfriend. We have never met.

'So you work for the people next door?' he asks.

So maybe Thabo Mbeki is right. But he is wrong too.

xiv

When finally it comes, it comes quickly. I had not even thought about it before.

'We can move to Cape Town,' I say to Justine.

xv

Black people just do not leave. They become nurses in London. They go off and work for investment banks in London. But they just do not leave. The last time I heard of it I was living in London. In June 2001, Dr Ike Ntsike-lelo Nzo, son of the late ANC secretary-general and former foreign minister Alfred Nzo, wrote in the *Sunday Times*:

In 1991, I came back to South Africa, after 26 years in exile, to explore the possibility of transferring my post-graduate psychiatry training from Sydney in Australia to South Africa. I was already two years into a five-year psychiatry programme.

During that exploration, I came across a doctor who probably thought of me as insane for contemplating returning. Inside, I was angry with him because I felt he was insulting my sense of patriotism.

Today, 10 years later, I am beginning to think that doctor was not far off the mark.

The criminals and criminality, unique to South Africa, have dealt a huge blow to my sense of patriotism.

I am now at a point in my life where I am agonisingly contemplating emigrating or going back into exile. Some people in the political world will be shocked and disappointed by this. After all, I am the only child of the late Alfred Nzo.

My late father was the longest-serving secretary-general of the ANC. He was the first black foreign minister of South Africa.

The idea of leaving South Africa for blacks is an arid desert, an unknown place of complex emotions centring on scorn, patriotism and the feeling that one has failed.

Every day now, I check the locks twice.

xvi

This is what has happened to me in Johannesburg in the past ten years. Three and a half of those ten years were spent elsewhere in the world. Another year was spent in Cape Town.

A gun was held to my head and my first car taken away when I had had it for only seventeen days. My flat was cleaned out. Two muggers chased me down the street in Braamfontein, knives gleaming in the sunlight. My neighbour defrauded me. My 1969 Mercedes Benz, bought specifically because I believed it had no value for thieves, was stolen. My house was broken into and valuables stolen. My wife and I were shot at in our bed. A burglar broke into the temporary flat we moved into in Killarney while we were sleeping and stole credit cards and a cellphone from our bedside table.

I also lost faith in the ANC, the organisation that shaped my view of the world.

xvii

My daughter Freya Onthatile is born on 22 December 2006. My sister Gloria is at home with our three-year-old, Ayanda. Justine's mum, Pat, and I are in the delivery room.

At 8.30 pm, while Justine is in labour, my phone rings. It is my sister. The alarm has gone off and she does not know what to do.

I am on the phone to the security company when Marinda, the midwife, comes to me in the corridor.

'You had better come here if you want to see your child born,' she says.

Freya Onthatile, fat baby girl with a slow smile, is born at 9.21 pm. I am so happy.

I call my sister, not to tell her about the baby, but to check if they are okay.

xviii

I check that the electric fence is working and I lock the doors. I put the beams on. I do this every day now.

My wife cannot bear to sleep in a room without an open window. I resent this. In the early hours of the morning, the alarm goes off.

I am glad of the sunrise.

xix

The first funeral I went to when I returned to South Africa in 2003 was at my mother's neighbour's house. The neighbour's daughter, who was exactly my age, had been brought home a few months before and had been bedridden since.

She died of AIDS. Her son was my thirteen-year-old nephew's best friend. I did not know what to begin to say to that boy. I gave him a football shirt.

Now three of my nephew's friends – all the same age – have lost a parent to AIDS.

Five million people are HIV-positive in South Africa. Only about 200 000 are on life-prolonging drugs.

The scale of the problem – the orphans, the old people left with children, the challenge to the state – takes my breath away.

Crime, at these times, seems almost a minuscule problem, a problem for those of us who twitter away at dinner parties.

This much I know is true: I am very afraid.

Me.

I am afraid for my daughters. I am afraid for my family. Me.

I am afraid. I lock the doors. I check the security beams.

Five million people are HIV-positive.

Beams. HIV. Bullets. Beams. Locks. I don't know which will kill me first: my insane mind, my despair, or a bullet from a stranger's gun.

XVX

The house I rented in Cape Town in 1997 is up for sale. Justine and I are very excited. 'Call them tomorrow,' I say.

It feels natural to be running away from our own, beautiful home, place of so many beautiful memories. It feels natural. I am astonished by this. It feels absolutely right.

Justice Malala is head of Johncom's magazine division. He is a columnist on the *Financial Mail* and *The Times* and is resident political analyst for e.tv. He lives in Parkview.

Brenda

Lara Allen

'Bring me a Magnum. The classic one, I don't want nuts.'

A Magnum! It's February and we are having a heat wave. But Brenda wants a Magnum – I will find a way. It's taken me months to get past the gauntlet of gate-keepers, jealous admirers and other hangers-on. Finally I've got to speak to her personally on the phone and have arranged a meeting. I'm not going to ruin an interview with the queen of township pop by arriving without the desired ice cream.

In February 1996 I was new in Johannesburg, trying to get my fieldwork going for my PhD on women in South African popular music. The city of gold left me bewildered. And for a long time the particular kind of gold I sought proved extremely elusive – gaining inter-views with famous musicians was not an easy or quick task. Gradually, however, as the word got out that I was not yet another journalist, promoter or music industry tout out to make a quick buck on other people's talent, musicians started to invest time and energy in my histor-ical project. Once a first meeting with a particular musi-cian was finally achieved my difficulties were generally over: communication was usually relaxed, generous and easy. Not so with Brenda Fassie. Our first meeting was confusing, and each subsequent encounter became more, rather than less, demanding – practically, emotionally and psychologically. Yet I couldn't dismiss her as just too much trouble: as a person she was too magnetic to forget, as a musician too important. So I found myself in a game without any understanding of its aim or its rules.

The Magnum test, for instance: was it a trial of my commitment to my project, an assertion of power over me, or the spontaneous, immediate demand of child-like desire? Probably, knowing Brenda, it was a complex, partially manipulative, partially unconscious strategy to see whether I would care for her, spoil her, and feed her insatiable demand for corporeal pleasure.

When I arrived for our first appointment she grabbed the ice cream carefully transported in an ice-box and skipped away in delight.

'You remembered! I *love* Magnums!'

She directed a beam from her brown, almond-shaped eyes directly into mine, pouted, and then laughed.

'I like you – you understand me.'

She turned and looked me up and down over her shoulder through long, false eyelashes:'I will give you an interview. Not today, another time. We are rehearsing. My band needs to work harder. But you can come to my home.'

With a dismissive wrist flick that belied the invitation she instructed: 'You can watch now – you will learn a lot.'

First test passed. And learn I did.

The last smudges of the ice cream devoured, I opened the rehearsal room door and Brenda the flirtatious little girl transmogrified into Brenda the maestro.

I squeezed myself between the wall and some out-of-work speakers. The downtown rehearsal room was sweltering – literally and figuratively. The way Brenda rehearsed her band brought back visceral memories of the atmosphere in an orchestra under the baton of a feared and respected conductor. The wariness and concentration of 90 people under a conductor who can detect when the second trombone is slightly flat, and who is quite capable of stopping and insisting that the unfortunate player retune in front of everyone, is quite palpable. The band looked like a herd of impala with a hungry lioness on the prowl: taut wariness, ready to take flight, but not knowing yet which way to run.

The number was upbeat. Brenda was gyrating provocatively, but the band was concentrating hard. La Maestress was clearly on the rampage this morning.

I thought it sounded great, but in the middle of a phrase Brenda broke off and stamped her foot. The instant silence was frightening.

She was down on her haunches. Nothing moved except her flicking tail. She pounced, and the rhythm guitarist came down.

'No, *ma bru*! You are a wimp. Where's your balls?'

There was a quiet titter – but no-one wanted to attract attention and become the next victim.

'Da da ra da ta ta. Da da ra da ta ta.'

He played the riff.

'No! No! Like this.'

She slammed down her microphone and leapt towards him, strumming an air guitar with great force.

'Da da ra da ta ta. Da da ra da ta ta! Play!'

'Da da ra da ta ta, Da da ra da ta ta,' she chanted with him, over and over again.

The guitarist was very young. His eyes were wide and fixed on Brenda, his whole being focused on the jaws of death.

'Da da ra da ta ta. Da da ra da ta ta.'

Clearly he wasn't getting it. Her face screwed up. Her body became more contorted and frenzied as she danced the riff. She grabbed a drumstick from the terrified drummer and I momentarily wondered whether she was going to demonstrate the rhythm on the unfortunate musician.

'Da da ra da ta ta,' she beat on the nearest amp.

The guitarist joined her. Again and again the riff cycled round.

The guitarist was sweating.

The band was completely still.

The universe was focused down to the embodiment of da da ra da ta ta as it was unfolding between his hands and her body.

Da da ra da ta ta, round and round and round.

Suddenly something shifted. Something sounded different. Brenda laughed and danced the riff like a happy child.

'Play!' she shouted at the drummer, throwing his stick back to him.

'Join!' she yelled to the rest of the band.

The lens of existence zoomed out to the wide angle of normality and the room returned to the number. No blood spilt today. The rhythm guitarist had survived; he would live to tell his lioness story, sprawled across bar counters relating his encounter with death to wide-eyed young musicians for years to come.

The extraordinary thing was that Brenda was absolutely right. Suddenly there was groove. Suddenly the number was completely irresistible. Everyone was beaming and moving their bodies as much as their particular instruments would allow. She had found that elusive active ingredient that turns a good song into a hit. She wanted a particular kind of attack, modulated and subtle, from the rhythm guitarist. She heard it in her head and she found a way of getting it out of him.

I was astounded. In a different time, in a different place, what could Brenda have done with that kind of musical facility, that subtlety of imagination, that finesse? She had reached the top of her profession. She was pushing her genre as far as it could go. What might have happened if women of her generation had had the opportunity to become producers? What if Brenda had had training in other musical styles?

What if Brenda had had a different personality? Many of her detractors assert that she created her own glass ceiling, that she dug her own grave. Even her most loyal fans have to admit that there is a great deal of truth in this. However, perhaps the myth that great artists are great because they risk more than ordinary people was true for Brenda? Perhaps the force within her that wreaked such destruction, in her life and the lives of those close to her, was also the force made her music extraordinary? Certainly this seemed true of the rehearsal I watched, and of the performance she was working towards.

That performance was *Brenda: Live at the State Theatre*, 11 March 1996, one of the first events to open the doors of that bastion of 'high culture' à la Afrikaner nationalism to black South African popular music and its audiences. It might have been projection on my part, but it seemed that the crowd's response to the song 'Black President' was a particularly emotional owning of that iconic space, the State Theatre.

It was a highly charged afternoon by all accounts. Brenda was in superb form. Striding around the stage in black thigh-boots she sang from the nucleus of every molecule in her body. Her searing vocal quality cutting straight to the heart, every phrase perfectly shaped for maximum emotional effect. The rhythm was irresistible and the auditorium rocked. Always provocatively sexual, Brenda's extraordinarily energetic choreography included high kicks, splits and backbends. Thank goodness for radio microphones! The band was tight, the lighting and staging slick and professional, the sound outstanding. Naughty imp, sophisticated seductress, petulant child, she carried us on waves of emotion, through hit, after hit, after hit.

The five-year-old girl next to me knew every word of every song. By the end of the afternoon, when the taller people around her took to their feet, she bounced on the flip-back chair so that she could see, and so that she could shout at the top of her voice: 'I love you, Brenda!'

We were all shouting that. Several times between numbers Brenda strode to the front of the stage to cry out: 'I love you! Do you love me?' Hands on hips she'd wait for our response. It was never enough the first time:

'Do you love me?' she'd scream.

'We love you, Brenda!' we'd bellow as loud as we could.

Momentarily she'd believe us. Her screwed-up face, devilish in anger, was suddenly transformed by delight. But everyone in that auditorium knew that we couldn't meet her insatiable demand. It would never be enough.

A few days later I finally got my promised interview. I was still having to pull over into side streets to consult my Johannesburg map book, and I was (rather unsuccessfully) pretending to myself that I wasn't afraid driving around alone in the centre of town at night going to gigs. My web of self-deception included bravura about being quite comfortable finding the homes of musicians in Berea, Yeoville and Hillbrow. In fact I was a lot more comfortable in most townships where people were generally helpful to bewildered whities lost because apartheid saw fit to save money on signposts in townships, and omitted such areas from map books.

Needless to say my interview with Brenda stretched me before it even started. I got lost in Hillbrow before finding her flat in Berea, but managed to arrive on time and without mishap. The block was in a relatively good state of repair, but the stairwell reeked with the stench of boiling cabbage. Mercifully the smell was significantly muted inside the flat.

There wasn't a lot of furniture in the lounge – a couch and a sound system on the floor. My arrival was somewhat overlooked because Brenda was haranguing her son Bongani about the fact that he had borrowed her car and returned it dented. Having had her say, however, she suddenly turned to me, beamed, and graciously invited me into the room where the interview was to be held: the bedroom.

She jumped into bed – still occupied by her beautiful young lover of the moment. He looked distinctly uncomfortable but understood, as did I, that we were required to play supporting roles in a cameo starring, and directed by, Brenda. Stars must have human reflective surfaces to confirm their lustre. Brenda required such acknowledgment and affirmation at all times. Fortunately for us both, she was still dressed in the apparel donned for an all-night recording session – a tight silver garment that would have suited a pole dancer in a 1970s sci-fi movie.

Actually I was grateful that the set for my scene was only the bedroom. Brenda was the self-styled South African answer to the American popular music star Madonna, and Madonna had recently given an interview in the bath! Like Madonna, Brenda courted controversial media attention. Apart from real circumstances of interest to the tabloids (her turbulent personal life, bisexuality and substance abuse, for instance) she often said and did things simply to attract attention.

'Yes, I say funny things sometimes,' she admitted. 'Because I know at the end of the day the motherfucker's going to write something that's going to make him famous – writing that about Brenda Fassie. So thank you to him! I purposely do that because I know exactly that's what happens. So why not?'

She knew why not though, for she wanted journalists to report only the outrageous statements or actions that she manufactured for that purpose. When the media exposed something she wished to hide she became extremely angry and unhappy. And she often had much to hide. Unlike Madonna, Brenda was in control neither of her own desires, nor of the media machine. And she was not hardened against the social implications of the bad-girl image that part of her worked so hard to create and maintain. Mostly she hated the press.

'They're all rubbish. They just wanna get rich by writing shit about Brenda. I'm a moneymaker, newsmaker – life goes on.'

She was lucky that I wasn't a journalist, because that day she was extremely out of it, and the only way of producing copy out of the interview she gave me would have been to sensationalise the effects of her addiction. She did have enough awareness to know that things were not going particularly well.

'I'm wasting time. Here you are coming to ask me questions about music and I am in such a fuckin' state.'

'You're doing fine.' I assured her. But I was beginning to wonder. The Brenda that had rehearsed her band with such clarity and assurance just a few weeks earlier, the Brenda that had had a State Theatre capacity audience hanging on her every phrase, had entirely disappeared.

The interview went all over the place: snippets from her biography that I knew already were interwoven with stories seemingly concocted on the spot for my entertainment. The latter were an impressively creative melange of fact and fiction. Within fifteen minutes I was emotionally seasick: churned around in a storm of feelings that rose in response to the kaleidoscope of emotional demands directed at me. I felt outrage, compassion, revulsion, shock, adoration and empathy – all at the same time. I was outraged and insulted that I was expected at least to pretend to believe such tosh, honoured that she was prepared to give me two hours of her life, embarrassed by her provocative sexuality directed simultaneously at me and her lover, attracted by her flirtation, frightened by her barely concealed urgent anger, saddened by her desperate yearning for love, alarmed by her erratic mental and physical state.

She darted around the room like a grasshopper throughout the interview: bouncing on the bed, searching in the cupboards, sewing a fringe onto her miniskirt, and talking volubly throughout. She was particularly fixated on stories of her childhood: tales of triumph and woe, cunning and wit, all featuring herself as the main trickster character and co-starring her childhood friend Tido Bam. Tido exists, and confirms that she and Brenda did bunk school together. But did they really contrive to push a teacher into a fish pond? Did they really pretend to be blind and sing for coins at Langa train station? Did Brenda tell the security police where her brother was when they put a gun to her head? Did she constantly steal money from her mother's purse to buy chocolate?

Ultimately, does it matter whether or not these or any of Brenda's other stories actually happened? What is truth in relation to someone whose mythological existence is of greater significance than what actually happened? Also, what was Brenda really trying to tell me by relating story after story of childhood naughtiness: how she always got what she wanted, even though she often got caught and punished; how being punished didn't really matter; how she would go to almost any ends for chocolate or other sweet treats; how she revelled in attracting attention, and breaking rules for the sake of it? Imaginative as some of the 'facts' clearly were, Brenda was, in a perverse way, being extraordinarily honest. She was revealing the fundamental characteristics of her nature, the basic desires and fears that have always motivated her.

I was overwhelmed by the sense that she needed from me, and from everyone else, more than any human was capable of providing. I suspect she turned the searing spotlight of that demand onto everyone who entered her domain. Part of me wanted to dash for the door, another part was mesmerised and fascinated by the contradictions. Mostly I was completely baffled.

After a long silence while she concentrated hard on her miniskirt fringe, she suddenly volunteered: 'You know that I'm asthmatic. You'd never believe me if you'd see me sick, you'd think I'm playing. Nobody ever believes me when I'm sick.'

She laughed, leapt onto her bed, jived to music inaudible to anyone else, and jumped back under the covers.

'Why?' I asked.

'Don't know. Everybody thinks I'm playing all the time. I always make jokes and they never take anything seriously. Next time they find me sick, you know, they'll find me dead. That's what they don't understand with me.'

The delight on her face as she related this scenario, the same delight as at the thought of the teacher in the fish pond, came back to me vividly eight years later.

'The South African superstar Brenda Fassie was

admitted to Sunningdale Hospital this morning following a serious asthma attack,' announced my car radio. 'Her condition is stable.'

In fact her condition was critical: she was in a coma from which she would never recover. Other truths seeped out slowly. The cause of her condition was not asthma but an overdose of crack cocaine. Further, she was not taken to hospital by her brother as first reported, but by her lesbian lover. The latter, it seems, was far harder for her family and spin doctors to admit publicly than the addiction that killed her.

The swing between outstanding artistry and an inability to function off the stage, well exemplified by the extreme contrast between her rehearsals and performance and the interview she gave me, characterised the rest of Brenda's life.

For five years running from 1998 she won the South African Music Awards prize for the best-selling album in the year of its release, and the album that featured her mega hit 'Vuli Ndlela' was the first South African recording to go platinum on the day of its release. In 1999 she won the Kora Award for best female artist in Africa. She has sold more than any other South African musician and is reputed to have earned more than R6 million in royalties in the last eight years of her life alone. More extraordinary than this exceptional commercial success was Brenda's artistic ability to move from one style to another, and remain at the top in both – a very unusual achievement in the world of pop music globally. The major star of 1980s township pop and disco, Brenda is widely credited as fundamentally influential in the birth of kwaito, and when her 2000 album *Nomakanjani?* went triple platinum, the press started calling her South Africa's kwaito queen.

The contrast with her private life couldn't have been more extreme. She went in and out of rehabilitation a number of times. Sometimes quietly, sometimes amid much media trumpeting and speeches from leading politicians. Inexorably, however, she sank into junkie hell. She moved from snorting cocaine to smoking crack, a habit that cost Brenda at least R2 000 a day, and South Africa a leading musician. She stopped breathing when she went into a coma and suffered brain damage. She died on 9 May 2004 and was buried in Cape Town on 23 May. President Mbeki addressed 20 000 mourners at her funeral in Langa Stadium.

It's 3 am two years down the line and Brenda won't let me sleep. But she won't let me write her either. My screensaver goes on again. I stare into the darkness of my safe, ordered, middle-class garden. In the shadows, just beyond my grasp, Brenda laughs. At me. With me. Teasing, derisive, flirtatious, perhaps very slightly encouraging, or is she just leading me on?

'What are you doing?' she asks. 'You can't write me down. It will be just like the rubbish all those other motherfuckers write. If people want to know about me, if they want the real me, they can listen to my music. Tell them to buy my CDs. Bongani needs the money.'

I am annoyed with myself. Why did I choose such a risky subject for this project? Out of all the musicians I could have written about, why did I choose the one with the most incomprehensible interview, the person I understand the least? Because my three brief encounters with

Brenda – an interview, a rehearsal and a concert – are burnt into the retina of my inner eye with such clarity, as if they happened yesterday; because I can't get her out of my head or my heart. And because I refuse to accept failure to do with anything work-related: I'm unwilling to admit that some kinds of understanding may be beyond my grasp. We all have our addictions, and it seems they get each of us in the end. Perhaps this is where I'm pushing beyond the possible?

'But I do want to understand, Brenda. I want to understand just a little bit more.'

She throws clues out of the darkness: fragmentary melodies; a disembodied rhythm; words, phrases, groups of words that are not phrases; bright eyes through long lashes, pouting lips; searing vocal timbre. Key words tumble into my consciousness, but without the joining phrases, without the connections that explain the relationships; without what's required for understanding, for analysis. Without what I need to do my job. The words of my screensaver morph into 'you are failing' and glide in technicolour splendour around my screen.

Fragmented words glide in from the garden: glittering stage, stinking gutter; extraordinary artistic success, catastrophic personal failure. Dagga. Cocaine. Disturbing, disruptive, bewitching, frightening, attractive, terrible, determined. Completely straightforward, absolutely controlling; brutally honest, sincerely manipulative. Mother. Star.

The differences that structure 'normal' life start to merge into each other. Daylight dichotomies seem illusory. Opposites contain each other. Exhausted and

confused I rest my head on my desk, crossing my arms
in an attempt to fend off the implications.

Silver miniskirt, black thigh-boots.
Chocolate ice cream, boiled cabbage.

Seduction,
desire,
need.

Brenda.

Lara Allen is a researcher at WISER, on secondment from the Wits
School of Arts. She is the author of articles on black South African
popular music, with a specific interest in women musicians.

Mirage

Fred Khumalo

'Hey, Khumalo, can you please spare me fifty bucks?' Vumindaba Dube moves his lips closer to my left ear, washing my face with fumes of stale liquor and other unmentionable things he has consumed, as he tries to whisper a request above the hubbub of voices in this crowded joint, 'Just twenty bucks, money for tonight's accommodation?'

Yeah, right, money for tonight's accommodation. A mantra that has been whispered in my ear numerous times by the polluted winds that blow up and down the crooked streets of Yeoville and Hillbrow.

I take another gulp from my drink. Kenny the television producer – or whoever it was, can't remember now – changes the CD in the music system. Miles Davis launches into 'All Blues'. My head nods to the familiar beat – dum-dee-dum, dee-dum, dee-dum. When John Coltrane takes his solo, I holler in appreciation. Mix beer and jazz, you get euphoric madness.

We are at Ekhaya & All That Jazz, a restaurant-cum-bar; more bar than restaurant. The food is an afterthought. Rubbery steaks and gritty rice. Shit. There is a fan whirling around and around in a futile attempt to banish the stale smells of the place. There's a huge poster of Miles Davis 'En Concert'. Good-looking black man. His presence lends a jivey mood to the place. This is Ekhaya. This is where many of us feel at home sometimes. You go north – Rosebank, Sandton and other 'leafy' suburbs – you are bound to pick a fight with people who, because you don't speak in hushed, pseudo-intellectual tones and you constantly complain about their bad music, think you are some kind of freak who doesn't 'belong'.

So you come to Ekhaya. At least here they let you be, allow you to tell it like it is.

While Yeoville, where the bar is located, is a haven for foreigners – Zimbabweans, Nigerians, Somalians, Ethiopians, Sudanese, et cetera – Ekhaya itself is frequented by South Africans. Black professionals including lawyers, writers, teachers, bankers, TV personalities and other more eccentric types who live in the northern suburbs but feel more at home socialising at Ekhaya, their Soweto in the heart of Johannesburg's inner city. Highly charged political and intellectual debates are on the bill of fare.

Ekhaya, which means 'home' in Zulu, has truly become a home from home for many young thinkers and professionals. Here you bump into Glen Mafoko, the bass guitarist; you rub shoulders with famous lawyer Zola Majavu, who consults for the Premier Soccer League; you share a beer with Mojalefa Gwangwa, the music promoter who has brought to this country such luminaries as Joe Sample and Branford Marsalis.

Brenda Fassie used to be a regular while she was still alive. So, you get the profile of the place, don't you?

Ekhaya sits cheek by jowl with Kin Malebo, a restaurant which is owned and frequented by Congolese nationals and is famous for its soul food and frenetic music. Opposite Ekhaya is 'little Lagos', a collection of cafés and pubs owned and frequented by Nigerians. Some of these foreign-owned cafés come and go, but Ekhaya is always there for South Africans to engage in the never-ending struggle with South African Breweries' green and brown bottles. And they talk. Do they talk!

Because of its location, Ekhaya does attract a steady flow of foreigners. But they never stay long enough to appreciate its personality. They come, they sip and they fly, as we say in township argot.

Dube is one of a very few foreigners who feel comfortable here at Ekhaya, among us South Africans. He is Zimbabwean. Intelligent chap. I've known him for, let's see, four, five years, give or take. Well read. Argumentative. Not very well groomed though. When I'm in the mood, I tell him: 'Bru, take care of those dreadlocks of yours; wash your clothes; a shower won't kill you; toothpaste doesn't give you constipation, nor will it make your teeth fall out; the white people were kind enough to think up an invention called lip balm, and a magical thing called deodorant.'

When I speak to him about personal hygiene, he merely laughs and shrugs: 'You don't understand. In order to survive in the streets, you must look ragged and destitute. The muggers will leave you alone.' Survival strategy.

Tonight I feel like throwing this hygiene-related jibe at him, just to shake him off.

But he is insistent: 'I'm not joking with you. I need money for tonight's accommodation.'

Now this gets me thinking. I seem to recall that on the many occasions that I have given him a lift home, I have always had to drop him at a different spot. Which means I don't even know where he lives, or what he does for a living. I know he's told me that back in his mother country he was a production supervisor. But here in South Africa … he just exists. I guess I've never given the matter a second thought because I don't want to burden myself with other people's hardships. I have heard many sob stories in this city which I have been calling home for the past eleven years.

In my mind I play back some scenes in which I have bumped into Dube. I spot him at street corners, see him at late-night bars – when I myself can't do the sensible thing and go home to sleep. He goes to nightclubs in Hillbrow, I'm told. Perhaps it is at these all-night clubs that Dube sleeps.

'If I give you the money, you promise you won't drink it?' I ask him now.

He shows me his teeth in what passes for a smile; but the emotion in his eyes speaks of a deep pain.

'If you don't trust me, please drive me to the place where I'm going to put up tonight. There you can personally pay the caretaker. I've known you for some time now, but I have in the past been too embarrassed to take you inside the places where I sleep. Come with me.' Just like that, he's thrown down the gauntlet.

That sobers me up; I decide to take him up on his offer.

After a couple more drinks, we get into my car and drive up Bezuidenhout and then into Wyndcliff. I'm traversing the dangerous twilight zone between sobriety and drunkenness. It's around midnight. He tells me to stop in front of an ancient-looking house. It used to be elegant in its time, that I can tell. But now most of the windows are broken. Pale light smudges the curtainless windows. There are ghosts of movement from inside one of the gaping window frames. We get out of the car. Dube leads the way.

The door opens readily into what used to be a lounge. The lighting is so weak that I stumble on a heavy object on the floor.

A voice groans angrily. As my eyes adjust to the weak candlelight, I realise that there is a mixed salad of humanity scattered all over the floor.

The next thing that hits me is the heat. I start perspiring. Men and women are speaking in hushed tones somewhere in the darkness.

Dube pauses ahead of me, waiting for me to catch up. We keep walking down a maze of passages. Odours arise: of stale sex, violence, urine, the stench of lost hopes, the stench of crushed dreams, despair, pain.

Further into the catacombs of the house, reggae music is booming. We succumb to the pull of the music.

At last we arrive at what seems to be our final destination. In years gone by, this would have been the master bedroom. A paraffin lamp flickers from a corner. A confusing festival of curtains has been used to partition this room, this cave, into at least three compartments. There are voices, noises from beyond these curtain partitions. Some of them are drunken voices; others voices of insomniac lovers teasing each other.

Finally, Dube parts a curtain. We enter into the brightest-lit part of this Balkanised room. Seated on a mattress is a man. A blanket covers his legs. He is naked from the waist up. He is smoking a joint. A woman is lying next to him, her face peering from underneath the blanket. She is looking at us.

'I didn't think you were coming,' the bare-chested man says, flashing a dark smile at Dube. 'It being a Friday I thought you would pass out in some bar.'

'*Awuzwe lo uthini* – listen to what this one is saying,' Dube responds.

Introductions are made. Without losing a beat, Dube launches into a sentence that takes away my breath: 'Khumalo, this is the caretaker, the guy you owe fifty bucks for my accommodation tonight.'

'No problem,' I say, trying to be casual. I proffer the required cash to the caretaker.

He accepts the money, walks out of the room, commands someone to go get some beer. A few minutes later we are drinking beer straight from the bottle. The caretaker smokes dagga. Dube tells me most of the people in the house are from Zimbabwe, 'Mugabe's children lost in the diaspora.' We drink some more. And more.

By the time I drive home the rising sun is casting purple silhouettes in the sky. Were we in a more relaxed, homely environment, the cocks would be crowing. But this is Johannesburg waking from a fitful sleep.

Saturday morning. Drunks are straggling home. Sober-minded people are walking, businesslike, towards the taxi rank, obviously going to work to earn a couple of rand so they can continue to maintain – just – their precarious existence in this dog-eat-dog city.

Dube is probably sleeping in that shelter, probably having anxious dreams about who is going to pay for his bed that night, and the next.

The next night at Ekhaya, I ask Dube to tell me his story. He had to leave Zimbabwe, he said, because he was being victimised by his Shona countrymen. He is Ndebele. He has been in South Africa for fourteen years – looking for work; sleeping on park benches when he cannot raise money to pay for temporary accommodation.

The jobs he has been able to land since his arrival in South Africa have not lasted – for a number of reasons.

'I came into a highly politicised and unionised environment, something I am not used to. I have refused to join trade unions, and that has landed me in hot water with colleagues who felt that I was a traitor, an *impimpi* who sides with the white employers. Difficult position indeed. I have worked at a number of places as a supervisor. In all the jobs that I have held here, my employers, who happen to be white, expect me to execute my duties without favour. My subordinates, who are black, want me to treat them with compassion. Sometimes they take advantage of the fact that I am a foreigner.'

This, along with many other challenges, has seen Dube moving from pillar to post. He has since started drinking heavily – and this is evident from his shabby appearance. Beyond the appearance, however, are a sharp mind and articulate tongue.

'I'm caught between a rock and a hard place. You see, in this country you need to have money for the usual reasons: you need money to eat; you need money for shelter; you need money to clothe yourself; but most importantly you need money to phone prospective employers, to send them e-mails or letters.'

Whenever he has differences of opinion with locals, they play the *kwerekwere* card.

'I felt alienated in Zimbabwe because I was in the minority, and in South Africa I feel alienated and insulted because I am a foreigner.'

Newly arrived individuals bring a complexity to the country. They are from all races, cultures. They bring with them skills and expectations, problems and solutions, challenges and wants. Which then raises the inevitable question: can we still continue to see blacks only as victims, and whites as oppressors; blacks as people steeped in vice because they are a by-product of a past that discriminated against them politically, socially, economically and otherwise, and whites as fat cats living off the sweat of the poor blacks? (True, some black fat cats have come to the fore, but we will burn that bridge when we get to it some day.)

Dube's story is a metaphor for this country which is fashioning itself a new identity. Generally regarded as a beacon of enlightenment in a somewhat dark continent,

South Africa therefore carries the burden of redeeming the entire continent and its children.

South Africa has the moral responsibility to open its heart and embrace other Africans who are seeking new horizons for themselves and their families.

Water flows because of gravity; people flow because of signs. And South Africa has that magnetic pull right now simply because it has signs that speak of hope and redemption. The colours of this rainbow nation are alluring, attractive.

The contradiction, however, is that for many foreigners, and locals as well, these signs of hope and redemption, the promise of a rainbow dream, seem like a mirage. You think you have grabbed yourself a slice of the rainbow, but then it recedes into the distance. And you keep chasing, and chasing, and chasing.

Fred Khumalo is Insight and Opinion editor of the *Sunday Times*, for which he also writes a weekly column. His novel, *Bitches' Brew*, was joint winner of the 2006 EU Literary Award. His autobiography, *Touch My Blood: The Early Years*, was short-listed for the 2007 *Sunday Times* Alan Paton Award.

A Prisoner's Wager

Jonny Steinberg

In February 2002 I went to the maximum security prison at the Pollsmoor Correctional Facility in Cape Town on a magazine assignment. There were four of us, three photographers and me. Our brief was open-ended. We'd go to the prison every day for two weeks. They would take pictures. I'd write.

By the end of our first day on the job I felt I'd been in the jail a year. We visited at least a dozen communal cells during the course of the day, and, in each, the prisoners lined up to see us as if we were doctors come to prescribe some rare and vital medicine. Everyone wanted to unload his story into my notebook. Each would stare at my pen as if it were a magical instrument that would transport his tales, and thus a piece of himself, over the prison walls and into the world. When we walked out of the prison that evening, I had more than a hundred pages of raw narrative in my bag.

That night, countless fragments of story chased one another around my head. I felt incompetent to deal with them. I had no tools with which to interpret them, for I knew nothing of the place from which they had issued – the prison itself. They were disembodied, and thus meaningless. I felt pretty much that way for the entire two weeks at Pollsmoor – a charlatan, an uncomprehending collector of tales.

*

One of those tales belonged to a prisoner I shall call Farouk Nali. I still have not deciphered the meaning of the story he told me and probably never will. And yet it has stuck in my mind for five years now, which probably means it's worth telling.

Farouk approached one of my colleagues early on our third morning in Pollsmoor in the corridors of the prison's awaiting-trial section. 'I think you want to talk to me,' he said, 'somewhere private.' He had about him a quiet authority that demanded to be taken seriously. My colleague arranged for us to meet him in the gym on D section at 1 pm.

By the time we arrived at the venue, several of Farouk's lackeys had assembled. A young warder stood at the door to the gym, opened to let us in, winked as we walked past him, then closed the door behind us. Inside, two large inmates stood motionless at either side of the entrance. They nodded at us expressionlessly.

Farouk himself sat alone in the centre of the room on an old wooden chair. He tapped his foot nervously, his elbow on his knee, his palm cupping his forehead. He was dressed like a clean-cut American kid – white sneakers and jeans, a T-shirt and baseball cap.

Only once we were seated around him did he look up. He was young – early thirties at most – his face pretty and youthful, the look of a fresh college kid, I caught myself thinking. Only his mouth betrayed something darker. It was wide and full and sculptured, and may have been beautiful on someone else. On him it seemed to express voluble pain.

He stared at each of us searchingly before speaking.

'Where do you want to begin?' he finally asked.

'Wherever you are comfortable,' one of us replied.

Farouk never got comfortable. His mouth twitched as he spoke. His foot tapped the floor compulsively. But it was not long before an extraordinary eloquence, a natural storyteller's eloquence, scooped up his nervousness and poured it into his talk.

He began with an early memory, from when he was three or four, of a violent confrontation between his father and his elder brother. His adult self transmitted the child's trauma via a taut description of objects, each exuding an aroma of youthful emotion: the rings on his father's fingers as the older man gesticulated, the reverberations of a wooden dresser as his brother stamped his feet, a fantasy of this adult fury tearing the house down.

Then came the story of his grandfather's death, a pious Muslim man. He described the stillness in the invalid's room, a silence he had not detected the previous day, the look of terror in the old man's eyes as he gazed at his grandson and saw his future – gangsterism and violence and an early death. He described the old man pleading with him to be a good boy.

As he spoke his grandfather's words, he began to cry. He kept his story going through his weeping, his voice broken and shaky, tears squeezing through the fingers with which he was covering his eyes.

At 2 pm, lockup time, the young warder who had

been standing at the entrance to the gym poked his head around the door and nodded. Farouk stopped, got up and walked out.

The following day, we found him waiting for us just as before, sitting alone in the centre of the gym. There was no warder guarding the door this time, and only one henchman.

'What do you want to talk about today?' he asked.

'Tattoos. Show us your tattoos and explain what they mean.'

He stood up and took off his shirt. His relation to his naked torso was surprisingly coy, and I immediately felt guilty, as if we were treating him like a circus animal, humiliating him subtly. He pointed to the four stars tattooed on each shoulder. 'I am a general in the 27s,' he said.

He sat down and looked at us enquiringly, waiting for a cue.

'Tell us the story of Nongoloza and Kilikijan,' one of us asked. Immediately, he began to tell us the story of the early South African bandits, and of how their tale forms the bedrock of prison gang identity in South Africa. He explained how Nongoloza formed the 28s, how Kilikijan split from him and formed the 27s, how the laws of the gangs are extracted from the story of their respective criminal careers.

His narrative was quite unlike that of the previous day. The episodes from his childhood had been exquisite. The gang myths, in contrast, were flat and lifeless. There were large holes, there were things that made no sense, the characters in the story were not people but empty emblems.

Throughout the telling of this toneless story, Farouk behaved as if the walls of the bare gym had ears. Every time he heard a noise outside the door he would pause, look up suspiciously and nod at the big man at the door. The henchman would step outside, and only once he had returned and nodded the okay would Farouk continue his story.

At one point, a warder walked into the room, whistling a light tune, oblivious to the tension around him. Farouk froze, followed the warder with furious eyes, then watched him leave. It took him some time to collect himself and continue.

*

After our second meeting in the gym, we sought the warder who had guarded the entrance to Farouk's makeshift domain the previous day. His name was Craig. We found him sitting alone on the steps outside the entrance to the maximum security prison, eating a home-made sandwich.

'Craig,' we asked, 'what's up with Farouk?'

'Love problems,' he replied with a broad grin.

'Love problems?'

Among the prisoners in Pollsmoor's awaiting-trial section were two transvestites, Angela and Lucille. Angela was immaculately groomed, her sexiness residing in her unwavering poise as she walked down a corridor crammed with loud, sweaty men. Lucille was broad-shouldered and bad-tempered, her eyes vacant, her skin made decrepit by the crack she smoked all day, and the smack she took at night to come down from the crack.

Craig told us that Angela had seduced Farouk. There was nothing unusual in that. 'All the queers go for the big Number men,' he said. 'The generals and the germistons and the inspectors; that is how they survive in prison, it is their route to safety, cigarettes and drugs. And Farouk hadn't had a fuck in months.'

So when Angela came to Farouk's bed in the dead of night, he turned back the covers and invited her in. It was to be a prison relationship: a naked, calculated exchange.

Strictly speaking, Craig told us, taking long pauses between sentences, staring out at the mountain with a studied, philosophical countenance, a 27 general is not supposed to have sex with a transvestite. The 27 general of gang mythology is a spartan, lonely figure. He carries in his head the rules of all three gangs – the 26s, 27s and 28s – and he corrects infractions of intergang law by spilling blood. He is a man of violence and of principle; the pleasures of money and of the flesh hold nothing for him.

But in reality, Craig continued, the real flesh-and-blood general of the 27s is just a human being, and a man at that; so a little bit on the side, a casual relationship with a transvestite whore – people turn a blind eye.

Craig finished his sandwich, chucked the wax wrapping in a bin and leaned back on his elbow. 'The problem,' he continued, 'is when the general falls in love: that, my friends, is certainly not allowed.'

The first signs of the love, Craig said, came when Farouk expelled the prisoner who slept directly above him, and pinned a white sheet across the length of the double bunk: a little love nest, a zone of privacy for the young couple. In the mornings, Farouk would accompany Angela to the cell's communal shower, the extent of its privacy a waist-high wall. The cell's occupants would awake to see the general soaping the transvestite's back – a scandalous sight.

'A 27s general cannot do that,' Craig said. 'He cannot fall in love with a woman who has a *piel* between her legs and parade his love around the prison. As I told you, he is spartan and violent; he is not a man of love.'

'What happens to the general who falls in love?' we asked. 'What do the 27s do with him?'

Craig grinned at us malevolently. 'Well, at the moment Farouk is the highest-ranking 27 in this prison. He is the boss. There is nobody here who can punish him. But the moment another 27 general steps into this place, both he and Angela are in big trouble. He will be stripped of his rank and have the shit beaten out of him. And after the punishment is done, he is nothing, a *frans*, a piece of crap.'

'And Angela?'

'She will be punished too,' Craig replied, 'for corrupting a general.'

'When is another 27 general coming to this prison?'

'Could be tomorrow,' Craig said, 'or next week or next month. Who knows? Your friend Farouk is living on borrowed time. What's driving him mad is he doesn't know how much time.'

Our subsequent meetings with Farouk took on a new, haunted quality. We listened to his stories about Nongoloza and about his childhood, and the love story in our heads gave his words new meaning. We saw him as a tired old general – he was only 32, so Craig had told us, but by prison gang standards we imagined he was a veteran – burned out, disillusioned with the loveless, arcane world in which he was steeped. He knew that his love was doomed, that the Number would destroy both him and his love, but he did not care. He would rather author his own tragedy than return to a world he despised.

'I used to believe in Nongoloza like a disciple believes in his God,' he told us during one of our interview sessions at the gym. 'Now, I hate the story. It is not beautiful: it is an excuse for bloodshed.'

And his exquisite recollections of his childhood – these, we believed, were his attempt to shore up the human being he was before the Number took him: his own personal reckoning, the development of an account of what had gone wrong.

Only once did we mention Angela. At the sound of her name, Farouk shook his head and grew agitated. He collected himself and changed the subject, talking aimlessly of his time at a small rural prison in the Boland.

The last time we saw him he wanted us to swear that we would put his portrait and his story in the magazine.

'Why is it so important to you?' one of us asked.

'Testimony,' he replied. 'I want for there to be a photograph of me with my real name and my real story. To you that seems simple. Yet it is something I have lacked my whole life. Do it, and you will be giving me a great gift.'

The editors of the magazine did, in the end, publish a shirtless portrait of him, the stars tattooed on his shoulders, his eyes dead, his mouth set in a grimace of pain. Under his portrait was a caption, 'Farouk Nali, General, 27s,' and a brief biography.

*

I returned to Pollsmoor eight months later and stayed, intermittently, for nearly a year. I had come back to write a book. Part of my motivation was annoyance. The place had been so ostentatiously inscrutable, so quick to wear its mysteriousness as an emblem, that I imagined the process of trying to understand it as an assault, or perhaps an act of revenge.

Farouk was long gone when I got back. His trial (for armed robbery) had ended unexpectedly soon and surprisingly well. He had been released some six weeks after we last saw him.

I didn't think much of Farouk during the next while. I was absorbed entirely in the present, putting myself to the task of getting to know the prison as best I could. But as I began to understand the place better, our encounters with Farouk started coming back to me, first fleetingly, then quite often. The more I learned about Pollsmoor the more disturbing his story became.

I began asking about him. It wasn't easy. He had not, it turned out, been a high-profile inmate. Most gang members I spoke to looked at me blankly when I mentioned his name. I had to describe his face and his tattoos before a flicker of recognition crossed their faces.

Farouk was not a general in the 27s, I learned. He was a mid-ranking member of the 26s. His four stars were those of a captain, not a general. Nor had he and Angela ever been lovers. She had seduced a 28 on her second day in the prison, and had slept each night by his side ever since. With the help of two inmates and a warder, Farouk had written and performed a tragedy with himself as protagonist.

His performance had been impressive. He had

turned the walls of his confinement into a personal theatre, replete with props and a supporting cast, and when the performance was over, the props disappeared. Indeed, by the time I got back to Pollsmoor, Craig had been transferred to the Department of Correctional Services parole office in downtown Cape Town. I bumped into him once, outside the parole office. 'What ever happened to Farouk Nali?' I asked. 'Farouk who?' he replied. 'Who are you talking about?'

One of the two goons who had guarded the door was still in Pollsmoor when I returned. 'Are you still in touch with Farouk?' I asked. 'No,' the goon replied. 'I don't even know where he lives.'

I marvelled too at the way he had used intimate material from his own life to make the performance real – the death of his grandfather, his tears – and at his wonderful imagination, conjuring, as he did, a heart-wrenching love story from the bowels of this loveless place.

Yet if that's all there had been to Farouk's story – an unhappy and wonderfully gifted man using us as an audience for whom to conjure an impressive performance – his tale would have been no more than an intriguing diversion. But in getting to know the prison better, I discovered that far more was at stake; in stringing us along, Farouk had in fact placed himself in grave danger.

Some months before our magazine crew arrived at Pollsmoor, a group of documentary-makers had been there. They made a one-hour feature on the prison which had been broadcast on national television, and thus into the prison itself. A host of rank-and-file gangsters had sat for the camera, and once it was rolling they had forgotten themselves. A low-ranking soldier had described his life as a judge in the 28s. A 28 *wyfie* had given an account of the blood he took to become a general.

In the wake of the broadcast, I now learned, each of these pretenders had been severely punished. One was beaten with a bar of soap wedged in a sock. He had lain in hospital for two weeks with broken ribs and a suspected punctured lung. Another had been stabbed in the buttock.

As a middle-ranking prison gang member, Farouk had to have known all of this. And yet he urged us with passion to publish his picture, his rank of 27s general in the caption, his biography in the text. He knew, too, that the magazine would be distributed in Pollsmoor after its publication, and that if he was still there he would be beaten and humiliated.

The more I thought about it, the more opaque Farouk's motives became to me. I mulled it over, allowing possibilities to settle freely in my mind. One was that he was deliberating raising the stakes attached to the outcome of his trial. I am not sure why, but an image came to me of Farouk in tortured dialogue with his God. He has pleaded to the heavens to be acquitted and let out of this awful place. What God, he asks, would want me to spend the next decade here? His God answers his prayers, tells him that he will not spend a decade here, that he will indeed be acquitted. 'Do you swear?' Farouk shouts. His God says nothing.

Farouk is indignant. 'Let's see exactly what your word means to you,' he dares. The magazine crew comes along and provides Farouk with an opportunity to put a wager on his God's word. He does all he can to get his picture and his falsehoods in the magazine. Now, if he is found guilty, he will be in prison when the magazine is published, and he will be beaten to a pulp. He is focusing his God's attention, or perhaps fortifying his own credulity: 'I did hear my God speak to me, and to prove it I am prepared to risk all.'

Another possibility presented itself to me. The awful climax of the theatre he and his supporting cast performed for us was to be his violent downfall and his humiliation. The suspense resided in the uncertainty of the timing of his fall. A 27 general could have walked into the prison the next day, or not until the next year.

There is an uncomfortable parallel between the fate that awaited him in the fiction he invented, and the actual fate that awaited him as a result of having invented the fiction in the first place. For if he had remained in prison when the magazine began to circulate, he would indeed have got the beating forecast in the story. Perhaps, I speculated, Farouk inhabited a borderland between performance and psychosis. He was orchestrating his own beating: the moment the bar of soap cracked his rib, he would truly believe he was a great war general paying the price for having betrayed the martial virtues for love.

Or perhaps he was merely seduced by our credulity. Having an audience see him as he was in private fantasy was so nourishing as to cause him to forget the future and the consequences that lay waiting for him there. He was so intoxicated by the present that his horizons simply vanished, together with awareness of his self-interest.

My speculations grew increasingly idle. It would be best, I thought, if I tracked him down and asked him what he had been up to. I got his address from the prison authorities. It was in Athlone. At about the same time, I was getting to know some Pollsmoor inmates who were members of the Americans gang in Athlone. I mentioned his name to them. They knew him well, they said, a troubled man, lots of torment inside, very quiet, very introverted. A loner. He was living in Athlone now, they said. It would be easy for me to find him.

I prevaricated. The more I thought about it, the more I wondered whether confronting him with my questions would not constitute an invasion of privacy. For whatever he was imagining when he staged his performance for us was surely between him and his supporting cast. To go to his home and tell him of the questions on my mind would be a little like walking in on a person masturbating, I thought, disturbing a connection between thought and deed that is rightly played out in private.

So I resigned myself to never knowing why Farouk had taken such a risk in talking to us. But if his motives remained obscure, he did illuminate something extremely important about prisoners and their stories. During my first stint at Pollsmoor in February 2002, I stayed up one night reading Herman Charles Bosman's prison memoir, *Cold Stone Jug*. There is a passage in it that is difficult to forget. 'Touch a long-term prisoner anywhere,' Bosman writes, 'and a story would flow from him like a wound. They were no longer human beings. They were no longer people, or living creatures in any ordinary sense of the word. They were merely battered receptacles of stories, tarnished and rusted containers out of which strange tales issued, like djinns out of magic bottles.'

Farouk taught me that Bosman was wrong about prisoners. He is right that they are dazzling manufacturers of tales, but it is not true that the prisoners themselves are 'merely [the] battered receptacles of [the] stories'. The prisoners are in fact the djinns. They emerge from their tales transmogrified, new beings. Farouk was my first teacher of a lesson I'd learn again and again at Pollsmoor: that in prison stories are as real as knives, the telling of them as much actions with consequences as any deed one can perform with feet or hands.

Jonny Steinberg is author of *Midlands* and *The Number*, both of which won the *Sunday Times* Alan Paton Award. His latest book, about a young Transkeian man's journey through the AIDS epidemic, will be published in February 2008.

What the Blood Remembers

Sarah Nuttall

My mother arrived from Cape Town on Friday night. I was so relieved that she was finally here. So that if anything happened she would be with me. On Saturday morning we went shopping. I bought some black trousers and a grey top made from thin material with flecks of colour in it. It was late March and the trousers and the top felt cool and breezy. As we made our way home with the bulky, shiny bags, I was thrilled with these new things because recently I hadn't had much to choose from in my cupboard. I was 39 weeks pregnant.

That afternoon the three of us, A, my mother and I, sat in the sun at the round table outside. It was late summer, and the Johannesburg light was bright but soft. We hadn't yet done very much to prepare for the baby. I had been busy at work and wanted to leave it as late as possible. Just to be sure. Well, but then again, about two weeks before, A and I had sorted through the small clothes we had collected and laid them in the cupboard we had chosen for her. On this Saturday afternoon, we talked about names. We thought of Mia Fabienne. We also built a mobile for her, so she could watch the shapes spin through the air.

In the evening we dressed to go out. I remember my mother looked so lovely, even though she said something that showed that she didn't think so. I did. She had two strings of beads on, amber. A was wearing a light-coloured linen suit, and his skin shone. I took a picture of my mother and A. A had his arm around her.

The next morning I sat with my mother in the sun, feeling quite heavy, quite slow. Mia Fabienne was probably a bit tired too after last night. Usually when I had my tea in bed she would protest. This morning she was napping a bit later than usual.

It was the day of the small party that our friends were to hold for us. A dressed in his light-green West African *boubou.* I wore the thin grey top and the black pants, and the air floated through the top and down my arms. Our friends gave us presents. I showed them the latest scans in which you could see Mia's big, round face and fat arms. I had put them in a book covered in orange silk. On page one. I would probably fill the book with other pictures or funny little things of hers as we went along. E gave us a big book with black paper meant for art drawings.

Afterwards, when the party was over, we were standing in the street about to go and E said that she hadn't been keen to have this party for us because it was best to celebrate once the baby had arrived – but that she had enjoyed it after all. I had enjoyed the party too, but I thought she was right when she said that. Don't celebrate someone's life before they've lived in the world. Although by 39 weeks, not much could go wrong now. E said she's just waiting for her grandfather to arrive tomorrow, and then she'll come.

She was right. On Monday morning I went swimming at the gym. I always did 30 minutes, and that's what I did that day. Then I drove to the airport to pick up my father. Now that he was here too, Mia Fabienne could come whenever she wanted. I'd have the people I was closest to around me.

That night, around 8 pm, I felt an infernal tiredness. I collapsed into bed, and fell into a deep sleep. Maybe the last bit of pregnancy was finally going to tire me, the way the books describe it. On Tuesday morning, labour began. A dropped into the office to do a few things and came back a while later. We timed my contractions. I felt relaxed, had a bath. Around 4.30 pm we went to the hospital.

We took the back route through Parktown North and then up through Hyde Park towards Sandton. The big dip in the road alongside the park in Parktown North, the thick rich green grass of late summer. I looked at the trees lining the street. Still now, two years later, when I take that route, the trees seem more alive than they actually are.

When we got to the clinic, I made my way to the labour ward. The nurse, who had seemed so nice when we met her before, was short-tempered. The doctor arrived and said that I was two or three centimetres dilated.

She will arrive at the unsociable hour of midnight, he said.

The contractions were getting harsher. He left. It was after 6 pm. My mother and A went off somewhere. The nurse put the fetal monitor on. She asked me to move onto my side. She seemed to think something was not right. She went out. My mother and A came back. They'd been filling in forms. Then the doctor came in.

I'm very sorry but I'll have to do a Caesarean, he said. Your baby is showing signs of fetal distress. She is not responding to the contractions as she should.

Okay, I said. It was not something I felt especially afraid of.

I'll do you at 7 pm, he said. I have another woman on the table, an ectopic.

'On the table'? Is that really how he sees his work, I remember thinking. It was 6.30 pm. He left. The nurse wheeled me into the corridor outside the room. Anxiety spiralled through me. I looked at my mother. I was wheeled down a corridor by someone I didn't know and parked there. A stood next to me.

People walked past us. The hospital seemed busy. No sign of the nurse. After some time, somebody else wheeled us further and left us somewhere else. A was asked to change into hospital gear. Someone parked the bed in a sort of side section, with curtains halfway around. Hospital staff walked past us. It looked like some were going off duty. I looked at them; I looked at A's face. I felt tense. Why was there such a long delay? I had no watch. Had I known the time, I would have known that it was after 7.30 pm. An anaesthetist came and gave me an injection in my back. I lay. A stood. Eventually someone pushed us through the back curtain into the theatre.

My doctor came in and said, Why do you look so nervous? It will be fine.

I didn't feel anything as they made the incision. I looked up at A's face. In ten minutes or so I heard a baby cry. The clock on the wall said 8.10 pm. The baby was taken over to a table at the side. I strained my head to see. A doctor was using what looked like bellows.

Is the baby all right, I asked into the ceiling of the theatre.

She's just a bit lazy, said the anaesthetist.

I asked again.

She's fine, my doctor said.

I was wheeled out of the theatre. And parked in a side room. After a few minutes my doctor came in. He was already showered and dressed in his brown leather jacket. I looked at him.

Is the baby all right, I said.

Your baby's fine, he said. But anyway, it's over to the paediatrician now, he added. He left.

A nurse wheeled me out of the theatre complex towards the lifts. I saw my mother and father sitting in two white plastic chairs outside the lift. My mother stood up and came towards me.

I don't know where my baby is, I said to her.

It took so long, she said. The lift closed behind me.

I was wheeled along another corridor. Into the ICU. My mother reappeared. I was shown a baby in a glass box with wire cords all over her. She was really big. She was very beautiful. I couldn't touch her. I looked.

She's very white, I said.

No-one answered. I was wheeled out again, into a small room with a single bed. I felt my way into a deep sleep. Something shocking had happened.

*

I had never really wanted to get married before my late thirties. Even when I was 25 I knew that. It was around then – in my late thirties – that I imagined that I would like to have a child too. My idea was always that I would live first, own my life. I wanted to feel that life belonged to me, as a person, a woman, before I gave life to someone else. Before I could really care for them as they deserved. Or be able to tell them what it was all about. There were some things I wanted to do, be, write. Before I could become the someone else I would need to be, to be someone's mother.

While this idea of my life was certainly true to my deep self, two things also shaped it. The first was that nothing big had gone wrong before. Nothing had happened to stop me in my tracks, to force me off the path I had set. Nobody had died, nor had I myself been deeply wounded. Hurt, yes, when my relationship in Oxford didn't work out. But I was the one who had left, come back to South Africa in 1995, a few months after my PhD was finished. The second was that I had never stopped – to look about. Of course I always looked about, but I never derailed myself, took a year off, wandered about. I went from school to a BA Honours, spent a year being SRC president, then did an MA then a PhD then a post-doc, then took my first post as a lecturer and then my job at WISER. In my mid-thirties I travelled more than I ever had before and, by 37, I had been to Europe, other parts of Africa, Australia, India, the islands of the Indian Ocean, North and South America and China.

And now it *was* time to get married. And have a child.

*

The next day, around 7 am, as on the two mornings after that, my doctor came into the small, ground-floor room in which I had been asleep, accompanied by a nurse. I was in a territory between sleep and wakefulness. He lifted my nightdress and prodded the Caesarean wound, which had a plastic covering taped over it.

Your wound looks fine, he said.

He left and went to the next room.

During the day I was wheeled back into the ICU. She lay in a different bed now, in a room on her own, and the lid was off. I sat with her and looked at her. It was as if she wasn't mine. I couldn't believe that she had come out of me. She must have been four kilograms. Her legs and arms were strong and she had the loveliest lips. Her face was not puckered like some babies. It was round and smooth and less white than the night before. But she wasn't mine. So this is what childbirth is like. I was amazed by her. But how could I love her when I couldn't touch her? I wrapped my summer dressing gown around me more closely.

In the evening, my brother, a paediatrician from Cape Town, arrived. My mother said to go with him to show him my baby. No, I said. A went with him instead. My brother said that she was beautiful and also that the first 24 hours are crucial in determining a baby's chances. During the night hours A and I tried to sleep, but A had to half lie in a chair alongside the bed.

When my brother came back the next day in the late morning, he was terribly sick. He was pale, and he could hardly stand up. His body looked as if it would fold beneath him. As if he was swaying on a boat at sea, struggling to hold on to an invisible rail. Sicker than I had ever seen him. We sat in the café downstairs. My parents didn't seem to realise how sick he was. I thought perhaps he was sick because he realised Mia wasn't going to be all right, sick with what he perhaps knew but couldn't say to me.

That morning a psychologist had been sent to see me at 8 am.

You shouldn't worry, he said, perched on the end of my bed while I struggled to wake. We've had over 50 cases of asphyxia in this hospital and the babies are always all right in the end.

It's not asphyxia, I could have said. Even though no-one had told me what it was.

Shame, such a beautiful baby, the paediatrician said. But she's a very, very sick girl, you know.

The psychologist must have known by the way I looked at him that I wanted him to leave.

*

Of course you can't just click your fingers and get married. A used to ask me when we were driving to the supermarket, When do you marry me? I always just laughed. For five years. Now suddenly I turned serious. On the morning of my marriage I felt very uncertain. Would he always be travelling and leave me alone with a child, which I now wanted? Neither of us liked signing those lawyer's papers you have to sign when you get married. The minute the ceremony was over, or even before, I loved it. I loved being married. I still do.

So does A. Let's do it again, he used to say in the months after that.

Six weeks later we were in Salvador de Bahia in Brazil in an upstairs open-air bar. I ordered a gin and tonic. And then put it down because I couldn't, wouldn't, drink it. I still hadn't got it. But I was pregnant.

*

Two more things happened. One on Saturday and one on Monday. On Saturday morning I woke alone in the clinic. The others had gone home and I had decided to stay one more night. I asked the nurse on duty to phone my doctor to come to see me. I hadn't seen him for two days, nor had a single conversation with him. He found me in the ICU, sitting next to Mia.

Why did you tell me my baby was fine when she wasn't, I asked him.

Because you can't tell a woman with her stomach cut open that her baby's not fine, he said. He never looked at Mia.

I've had to pull out my textbooks, he said. And look, I've got to go to a wedding tomorrow, I'll see you on Monday. He left.

The other thing was on Monday. I spent the whole day with Mia on Monday and we were getting very close. I had fallen in love with her. I was even aware of what clothes I had put on that morning, because now I was someone's mother, I had to look good. I had to dress properly for her. She was my daughter. The grey flecked shirt and black pants and sandals. I had by now worked out a way of putting my head next to hers, even though the glass railing of the ICU bed cut into my neck. I could lay my hand on her chest between the cords. And on her head.

Her head was swollen at the back – the only sign that any-thing was amiss. I laid my hand on the back of her head for most of that day and said to her, Today, we're going to work on your head. We're going to heal your head.

The most peculiar thing happened. At 3.30 pm I felt a strong current course down my arm, the arm that was resting on her head. It was a quite discernible energy force. Two people, to whom I was not especially close, one in Cape Town and one in another country, became present to me. They would have called it prayer. To me it was an energy made visible for a moment, one of the higher layers of our being in the world. Layers that fold together with an intricacy beyond our usual under-standing but which on occasion reveal themselves to us. It was a confirmation of a life force whose power I have not felt so close again.

I was still there at around 9 pm. The paediatrician came in.

What time is the CAT scan tomorrow, I asked him.

We're not going to do a CAT scan, he said.

That's odd, I thought. I had planned to go along with her.

Then he said: But I'll tell you this: the swelling on her head has gone right down. Such a beautiful baby.

He left.

That night I went home and lay in my own bed. Suddenly I knew. For myself. It was over. She was going to die. After the doctor had left, I had said to the nurse, Why do you think they aren't going to do a brain scan?

Because they already know what they need to know, she said.

In bed I recalled that, but it was really the way the

paediatrician had said 'such a beautiful baby' instead of something else that made me know in the muscles and ventricles of my heart that it was over.

A meeting had been set for 10 am the next day. It was to be the paediatrician, my parents, A and me. In a small room adjacent to the ICU. We waited. He was late, and a call came through to say he was still in theatre. I lay with my head next to Mia, and I spread my hair on her chest. We were the closest we had ever been. Waiting for him was like waiting for nothing. It was only her and me. When he came I stood up. He signalled for us to proceed to the room at the end. The others started off. I stopped him.

Don't hurt them, I said. He looked at me and I could see that he knew then that I knew. I refused to leave the small room where Mia Fabienne lay. A came back. My parents had gone into the room.

I don't want you to hurt them.

He looked at me. I took A in my arms and held him tightly.

The paediatrician said: Your child has third-degree damage. She lost too much oxygen. She cannot survive.

I carried on holding A. He held me. We sat like that in the plastic chair. The paediatrician went to tell my parents. After a while, I got up and walked out of the ICU. I took the stairs and walked out of the hospital. I found a place where some water was falling, near the entrance, and I sat down next to the water, in the sun. If the eternal emptiness of shock could have a texture, be a substance, that was what I was now made of. No tears. Only the water falling, and the sun, and me.

*

The strange thing was, I didn't experience depression after Mia's death. Other things happened instead. I searched for her, then I felt almost manically alive, I suffered post-traumatic stress and, exactly two years later, I knew I had recovered.

Mia died on a Tuesday, seven days after she was born. On Sunday it was my father's seventieth birthday. We drove out into the country and had lunch looking across hills into the far distance. After lunch we went for a walk. I remember stopping and saying to my mother: Where is she? I don't know where she is.

It was the strangest feeling. As if she was just a hair's breadth away. Almost with us. It was like that for quite some time, in fact for what I later realised was close to 40 days, the time Buddhists say that the spirit of a person remains, before they are fully gone. This must be especially true when you have carried that person inside your own body.

About six weeks later V and P came from the United States to visit. I was thrilled to see them and I remember around that time feeling madly alive. I'd had this feeling once before, when my relationship with J had ended, though not as intensely. As if when something traumatic happens, it wakens you to another level, and the beauty and pain of life light something inside you. A and I drew very close and I knew that I had never been happier with him, with someone, in my entire life. I wanted to dance, go out every night, live.

Later I remember being at D and M's house one night. The conversation at the table turned to the subject of death. People were discussing Jewish attitudes to the dead. My head started to spin. I went and lay on the couch. My body started shaking uncontrollably. I don't know where she is, I said again. I remembered that they had not been able to find where her blood had gone, when she was so white after her birth. For three days they searched. This the nurse told me one night. Eventually they sent me for a blood test and found that her blood was in my blood. Returned to me. Later I found out more, for myself. I had several of those panic attacks, and each time I was in a space in which I was lost, unable to know what had happened and why, and where she was.

For many months I wavered between explaining to her in my head that I needed to be all right, to go on with my life, to be happy with her father – I needed her to understand that she was gone but not forgotten and I was here, in the world and had to live life, to be fine again – and blaming myself for her death. This latter is I think something deep in the unconscious of womanhood. I thought for quite some time that her death must have been because I worked too hard during my pregnancy, because I went on long flights to New York to teach at Yale across the middle period, because I didn't attend to her fully enough in my self, make enough room for her in my life – and so she left. This despite the truth that I rested every night after 6 pm, that many women fly long distances during pregnancy, that most women hardly know what's coming in their first pregnancy, cannot properly imagine that there really is another human being inside of them. I thought perhaps there was something strange about me, that I was too intense, that I was the wrong woman to carry a baby.

It was the greatest relief when in one of my conversations with myself I said one day: It just happened. In other words, it was nothing you did or didn't do.

With that came the beginning of a sense of letting go.

About six months after her death I exploded with anger and wrote a letter to the doctor telling him what I thought of him. An anger that stayed with me over several weeks, perhaps months, and which temporarily lost its main object and spilled into some of my friendships too. Since then, I have gradually lost that anger. I still think that had we not waited an hour and fifteen minutes for an emergency Caesarean, things might have been very different. Now I feel resigned to the fact that another's error can so much affect one's life.

On the first anniversary of Mia Fabienne's death, I lay on a mountainside with A and between 6 and 8 pm I relived labour, and the awfulness of her birth. My body felt very strange, inhabited, as if at the level of its cells, by traumatic memory. After 8 pm it began to pass and we had dinner together and slept well.

The following year, 2006, two years after her death, we were on Camps Bay beach in Cape Town, in the evening. After a while we sat on the rocks and seagulls screeched and squawked all around us. Small children played in the late light. I took out the picture of Mia I had put in the pocket on the leg of my trousers. We'll never know what happened to her, A said. I felt sadness for Mia, saw her beauty, but I felt light, and nothing, no force, clutched at my heart. I felt that it was just me, just us and that she was fully gone. Things were ordinary again. I knew then that in some important sense I had recovered.

That night we had dinner with my brother and sister-in-law. They both happened to talk about Mia and S said she thought about her every day.

You shouldn't, I said in my head to her: I don't.

My brother said that she may come back in unexpected forms and cause me emotional turmoil.

Maybe, I said, but actually I'm over it now, and I know that that is so.

They both looked at me. But it was true.

*

What happened to Mia and me is known, in medical terms, as a fetal-maternal haemorrage. Very few cases have occurred across the world. Medical science can explain little about how or why it happens. Quite commonly, very small volumes of red blood cells escape from the fetal blood system across the placenta into the mother. On the rarest of occasions one of two things can happen: a larger, slower process causes the fetus to lose more blood and to become anaemic and in danger, or a massive and instant bleed from fetus to mother can occur, of more than 150 millilitres, a tiny amount by the standards of an adult body – but enough to be fatal for a very small child. This could occur during a labour contraction. I found this out, with the help of my mother, by taking out several books from a library.

Perhaps, then, on the very day of our small party, Mia began her departure. Or perhaps, because her head had by then dropped low and ready for birth, she was simply able to move less than usual. Maybe, when we were lying in that corridor for all that time, and my anxiety levels suddenly rose, one of the contractions caused a bleed that was to be fatal.

Several months after her death I discovered that 7 pm is shift-change time in South African hospitals. As we lay in that corridor, it was really like lying in a bed on a street, as staff prepared to drive to their Sandton homes or to catch taxis to Alexandra and Soweto, and others arrived for another night on duty at the hospital. Certainly our nurse had been keen to leave. And no-one had appeared in her place. As the traffic on the hospital street grew, a small girl whom we had created and nurtured for nine months lost her chance at life, slowly like a fading light bulb, or quick as a flash.

Sometimes in the months following her death, I used say to myself that perhaps Mia Fabienne was quite a special sort of person, a strong presence, and that she herself had something to do with her slipping away, that her leaving was somehow in part of her own voli-tion. That she retreated in the moments before her birth to another layer, a world adjacent.

As I began to heal, I focused more on the fact that she was gone. Gone. I knew her only through the beauty of her physical form. For the rest, she remained, after the first loud cry she gave as she emerged from me, a figment of who she was or could have been. She opened her eyes several times. She had a look of extreme peace, helped perhaps by morphine. I used of course to think about her head, her brain. I thought that she probably had a good brain, and a lively imagi-nation already at work, processing sensations, recognis-ing sounds, coordinating her body, and steering her by then formed personality and character. As she lost that tiny amount of blood, she lost oxygen and that intricate work of mental and emotional life was shattered. Gently, I hope. Or was it violently?

Usually I would see my doctor on Mondays during that last month. That week, week 39, after the party, he changed it to Wednesday because of a busy schedule. Imagine if it had been Monday as usual. Would we have seen a sign? Beyond what a late scan might have shown, Mia herself never gave a sign. Perhaps, then, it all happened in an instant – in the moments before birth?

None of this entangles me as it did then. What remains more fully is the paradox of pain: that you would never have wished this to happen, but, having happened, it deepens you beyond doubt or return. Brings with it the tangible feeling of having gained a quickening of human being. This at least is what is bequeathed.

Sarah Nuttall is a senior researcher at WISER. She is the editor, most recently, of *Beautiful-Ugly: African and Diaspora Aesthetics*. Her daughter Léa was born on 12 July 2006.

Afterword

There is something immediate and unforgettable about the experience of reading these stories. It must be the honesty and integrity of the voices that tell them. It must be. Each voice is conscious of balancing on a wave of transgression. It dare not lose balance and threaten what could be the onset of another decisive moment in the lifetime of a new democracy. Believability is at the core of managing the risk of self-exposure. Each voice must reveal and retain dignity all at once. In this each voice seeks to assert the weight of personal testimony against the power of evocative futures which have suddenly and distressingly become the past.

Collectively, the voices behind these remarkable narratives help us to recall just how harsh the public space in South Africa often is. The news media tell it all: crime; corruption; grinding poverty; conspicuous consumption; new graveyards filling up with the AIDS dead; disrespect going under the name of comradely informality; criminality in schools; no-go areas in the politics of posture and recurring declarations of comatose manifestos; racial fiefdoms in the farms of the land; the enduring and indecent apartheid landscape;

abounding self-indulgent litigation; constant attacks on individual and institutional bona fides. It is a long, unrelenting, jagged terrain.

It is when viewed against such harshness that these personal narratives together become a profoundly radical statement. They have entered a public domain that is used to the dramatic and huge brushstrokes of political posture. This is not a world that accommodates niggling personal truths of the kind brought into the open by these narratives. How can anyone forget the personal experience of violence as described by Justice Malala in a country where the social pervasiveness of violence is officially downplayed? In this connection, the strength of these narratives is in the fact that they seek not to embarrass, as such, but more importantly to bear witness. The personal experiences become niggling truths habitually denied officially. It is through denials of this kind in so many other areas of public life that hypocrisy assumes a public form. The more pervasive the hypocrisy the harsher public life becomes.

These narratives express the capacity of the personal, intimate experience to soften the abundant harshness of public space and perhaps to introduce and affirm honesty and sincerity as public values.

These are not sentimental narratives. They engage the harshness of their lives, acknowledging it, often in wrenching ways. What is new about them is how they lay bare and equally acknowledge personal fears, vulnerability, doubts, desires, and agonies of conscience, as an expression of freedom. They offer us the possibility to expand our sense of freedom beyond the experience of knowing we have had it for thirteen years. Expanding our sense of freedom means having the ability to sense, to recognise and to know that precise moment when thirteen-year-old solutions may themselves have become new problems of the day. 'Welcome to the new problems of being ourselves,' the narratives seem to say to us.

To recognise that old solutions may have become new problems is not to strip old solutions of their value, but to historicise them. All solutions have a beginning and an end. History protects their value. Their (often unthinkingly) enforced permanence into a continuous presence is illusory and almost always devalues them. We only need to be aware that in the modern world, futures quickly become pasts.

This book takes us closer to the notion of 'making public spaces intimate' by infusing into the public domain, not gossip, but genuine, reflective, if sometimes agonised, personal testimony. Self-exposure of this kind is harder than the act of unmasking others. It allows for the public sharing of vulnerabilities as the basis for the restoration of public trust (against public hypocrisy) and makes possible a world of new, interpersonal solidarities that extend into broader, more affirming social solidarities.

The Truth and Reconciliation Commission hearings tried, among other things, to take us to the point this book seeks to take us to. Too soon, perhaps! We need to be disappointed first: disappointed by the increasing gap between our personal experiences and official denials of them. The value of disappointment is that its sources are as demonstrably human as these narratives are. From this perspective, disappointment becomes intriguingly restorative. It has given us a harvest of stories that can be seen to signal the onset of renewal.

At risk! In rough terrain, often harshly dominated by a future still being pursued and officially evoked to secure our compliance, the greatest risk is to be misunderstood. Honesty becomes a shield. But there are degrees of risk. The first risk is to expose a condition. Each and every one of these narratives does so. The second is to transgress. This is harder. The stakes are higher. Each narrative is also a transgression. The danger feared, and to which the narratives are a response, can either be confirmed or it dissipates. I sense that it will dissipate as a new South African sensibility emerges. The new world of the genuine personal experience will not be easy to ignore. Each and every one of us desperately desires it at this time. We are entering the most formative moment of our democracy. Navigating through this period successfully will lend sustainability to our next future.

Njabulo S Ndebele
Cape Town 2007